WANDA BRUNSTETTER'S

Amish Friends
NO WASTE
COOKBOOK

More than 270 Recipes Help Stretch a Food Budget

BARBOUR

Introduction

During my growing-up years, my mother was always frugal when it came to using the food she cooked for more than one meal. Leftover baked meatloaf that we'd eaten for supper became cold meatloaf sandwiches for lunch the following day. Nearly every chicken dinner gave us leftover chicken meat, which Mom used in homemade noodle soup, stir-fry, or a chicken-based casserole. Pot roast on Sundays meant cold roast beef sandwiches on Monday or vegetable-beef soup for Monday night's supper.

My Amish friends are also prudent when it comes to not being wasteful with the food they prepare for their families' meals. Leftovers are used wisely, and a meat dish for supper might end up being used the following day in a tasty homemade soup, potpie, or casserole dish or for sandwiches. On several occasions, my husband, Richard, and I have been invited to share in some of those tasty meals.

Within the pages of this new cookbook you will find many recipes and tips from Amish and Mennonite women who were pleased to share how they cook with no waste. I hope you will enjoy reading each of their contributions.

A big thank-you goes to my editor, Rebecca Germany, for compiling the recipes and tips that were submitted.

—Wanda E. Brunstetter

TABLE of CONTENTS

Advice for Surviving Hard Times – Less Is More

If the children are young and hubby is willing, cut a lot of things out and remember that less is often more.

Cut out baking. Small children don't even know that some folks have dessert at every meal. Rather than eating something like rhubarb at every meal (with oatmeal for breakfast, cobbler for lunch, and cold bread soup for supper) just because it is in season, do without that second course. Remember, sugar is very hard on teeth, and our culture has far too many sweets anyway.

Serve meals that are time-saving and filling. Breakfast should be eggs primarily; then if available, add meat and cheese. Keep pancakes, waffles, biscuits, and the like as a special treat. In the long run, whole foods such as eggs, meats, dairy products, and good healthy fats actually result in a much lower grocery bill, providing that you grow at least some of those things yourself.

Keep a cow and some chickens if possible. Eat veggies that are in season. Instead of canning endless rows of foods, grow food that keeps through the winter like potatoes, beets, carrots, onions, cabbage, sweet potatoes, and dried beans. Keep in mind that millions of people live on rice and beans—maybe not the best diet but undoubtedly healthier than the American processed food trend.

Fruits can be frozen. We grow berries and buy blueberries. Remember, though, that even fruit should be eaten in moderation and not necessarily at every meal. Especially moderate use of fruits canned with added sugar.

If you eat a diet high in healthy fats and whole foods, you may find that you don't crave processed junk foods as much—and save money.

Most of this advice comes out of necessity for a busy farmer's wife. I couldn't keep up with chores, laundry, canning, and baking, plus my three preschoolers, so I discovered that less is more. Less food and less things to manage results in more. More quality time. More relaxing moments in this busy life.

May God bless you all as we journey through this life.

S. Beiler, Woodward, PA

BEVERAGES

Come unto me, all ye that labour and are heavy
laden, and I will give you rest. Take my yoke upon
you, and learn of me; for I am meek and lowly
in heart: and ye shall find rest unto your souls.
For my yoke is easy, and my burden is light.

MATTHEW 11:28–30

Refreshing Peach Tea

1 cup sugar
7 cups water

3 cups sliced peaches
3 to 4 black tea bags

In saucepan, bring sugar, 1 cup water, and peaches to a boil. Reduce heat to medium and stir mixture constantly, crushing peaches as you stir. Turn off heat; cover and let sit for 30 minutes. Boil 6 cups water and brew tea. Let steep for 5 minutes. Remove tea bags and refrigerate until chilled. Strain peach mixture through strainer to remove fruit pieces. Add to tea and serve over ice.

Sadie and Edna Beiler, Ronks, PA

Iced Tea Concentrate

4 cups water
1½ quarts tea leaves, tightly packed
¾ cup honey

Boil water and add tea leaves. Turn off heat and let steep for 15 minutes, then strain. Add honey, stirring until dissolved. Put in freezer boxes. Mix 1 part concentrate to 3 parts water.

Sarah Stutzman, Homer, MI

COFFEE CONCENTRATE FOR A CROWD

5 cups coffee grounds
7 quarts cold water

Mix coffee and water and let sit for 2 days. Strain. Put in canner of hot water.
Heat and serve.

RHODA MILLER, Decatur, IN

ICED COFFEE SYRUP

¾ cup instant coffee
1 cup sugar

2 cups boiling water
3 tablespoons vanilla

Mix coffee and sugar; add boiling water and stir until dissolved. Add vanilla. Cool.

To serve, use ⅛ cup coffee base to 1 cup cold milk.

ALMA I. SCHWARTZ, Stanwood, MI

ICED COFFEE

¼ cup coffee
2 cups hot water
½ cup sugar

¾ cup brown sugar
½ cup caramel syrup
1 gallon milk

In gallon jug, combine coffee, hot water, sugar, brown sugar, and caramel syrup. Mix until dissolved and cooled. Add milk and fill pitcher with ice when ready to serve.

FANNIE MILLER, Pierpont, OH

Maple Mocha

12 cups milk
4 teaspoons instant coffee
Dash salt

4 cups hot water
2 teaspoons vanilla
¾ cup maple syrup

In saucepan, slowly heat milk. In bowl, dissolve coffee and salt in hot water. Add to milk with vanilla and maple syrup. Serve hot, or cool and serve over ice.

Mrs. Monroe Miller, Blanchard, MI

Cozy Hot Chocolate

¼ cup cocoa powder   1 cup water
½ cup sugar   ½ gallon milk

In saucepan, bring cocoa, sugar, and water to a boil for 1 minute. Add milk and heat through. Serve hot.

Anna M. Schwartz, Willshire, OH

Chocolate Milk

½ cup cocoa powder
⅓ cup evaporated cane sugar
½ cup milk

Whisk all ingredients together until smooth. Store in refrigerator. To use, add 1 to 2 teaspoons to glass of milk.

Hannah Hochstettler, Centreville, MI

Eggnog

3 cups milk
2 eggs

1 teaspoon vanilla
2 tablespoons maple syrup

Combine all ingredients in pitcher and beat until foamy.

"We live on a small farm where fresh milk and eggs are always plentiful. A meat and cheese sandwich plus a tall glass of eggnog makes an easy meal on a busy summer day. Add a scoop of ice cream to each glass of eggnog for a treat."

Barb Fisher, Ronks, PA

Homemade Root Beer

2 cups sugar
¾ tablespoon yeast
3 tablespoons root beer extract

Combine all ingredients in gallon jug and fill with lukewarm water. Do not put lid on tight. Let sit overnight in warm place. The next morning, put in refrigerator. Ready to drink when chilled.

Katie Zook, Apple Creek, OH

Orange Smoothie

1 (12 ounce) can frozen
  orange juice concentrate
2 cups milk

1 teaspoon vanilla
10 ice cubes

Mix all in blender and blend until smooth.

Katie Zook, Apple Creek, OH

Frothy Pumpkin Drink

2 to 3 eggs
1 quart pumpkin
2 cups milk
¾ cup sugar

1 teaspoon vanilla
1 teaspoon cinnamon
½ teaspoon salt
Whipped cream (optional)

In bowl or glass pitcher, beat eggs until foamy. Add pumpkin, milk, sugar, vanilla, cinnamon, and salt. Beat until frothy. Serve with whipped cream on top.

Julia Beachy, Salisbury, PA

Old-Fashioned Energy Drink

1 quart warm water
1 tablespoon fresh grated ginger
   or 1 teaspoon ground ginger

3 tablespoons apple
   cider vinegar
3 tablespoons maple syrup
Lemon juice to taste (optional)

Mix all ingredients and enjoy.

Fannie Gingerich, Navarre, OH

GRAPE PUNCH

1 quart grape juice
¼ cup lemon juice
½ cup cranberry juice

1 (12 ounce) can orange
juice concentrate

Combine grape juice, lemon juice, cranberry juice, and orange juice in 1-gallon pitcher. Mix. Add water to fill pitcher (or use less water if you like it strong). A great drink during cold and flu sickness.

KATIE ANN FISHER, Christiana, PA

BREAKFAST

*Let prayer be the key to the day,
and the bolt to the night.*

AMISH PROVERB

Heartland Cereal

3 sticks butter
1 cup honey
1 cup brown sugar
2 tablespoons peanut butter

10 to 11 cups oats
1 cup wheat germ or bran
1 cup coconut
¼ teaspoon cinnamon

In saucepan, melt butter, honey, brown sugar, and peanut butter. In bowl, mix oats, wheat germ, coconut, and cinnamon. Pour warm mixture over dry mixture and mix well. Spread on cookie sheets and bake at 350 degrees for 1 hour or until browned.

Sadie Zook, Taneytown, MD

Healthy Granola

4 cups quick oats
2 cups flax meal
½ cup coconut
¼ teaspoon salt
½ cup chopped pecans
½ cup chopped almonds

¾ cup honey
⅔ cup coconut oil
1 tablespoon maple
   flavoring (optional)
Cinnamon to taste (optional)
1 cup raisins

In large bowl, mix oats, flax meal, coconut, salt, pecans, and almonds. In saucepan, melt together honey and coconut oil. Mix in maple flavoring and cinnamon. Add to oat mixture and mix well. Spread in roaster and bake at 325 degrees for 20 minutes, stirring every 5 minutes. Add raisins before mixture cools. To keep granola fresh, put in canning jars while still hot, affix lids, and store jars upside down in cool place so they seal.

"This is very good. We have two children on a special diet that can eat this. We have made other granola for the rest of the children, but they would rather eat this."

Elizabeth Swarey, Charlotte Courthouse, VA

Pumpkin Seed Granola

½ cup pumpkin seeds
½ cup sunflower seeds
½ cup sliced almonds
½ cup cashews
2 tablespoons unsweetened coconut (optional)
2⅔ cups quick or old-fashioned oats

1 cup oat bran
2 tablespoons toasted buckwheat (optional)
½ cup dried fruit (figs, mango, papaya, banana, etc.)
½ cup raisins
½ cup dried apple rings

Put pumpkin and sunflower seeds in food processor and pulse to chop coarsely. Put in dry skillet and heat until lightly toasted but not browned. Transfer to large pitcher and let cool. Put almonds and cashews in food processor and pulse to chop coarsely. Put in dry skillet and add coconut; heat until lightly toasted but not browned. Transfer to pitcher and let cool. Add oats, oat bran, buckwheat, dried fruit, raisins, and apple rings. Stir well. Store in airtight container. Serve with milk, honey, or sugar. Yield: approximately 8 servings.

Elizabeth Swarey, Charlotte Courthouse, VA

Freezer Granola

35 cups oats
15 cups cornflakes or
    crisp rice cereal
7 cups whole wheat flour

3½ cups butter
3½ cups honey
5 cups peanut butter

In bowl, mix oats, cornflakes, and flour. In saucepan over low heat, melt together butter, honey, and peanut butter. Pour over dry mixture and stir to coat well. Put into airtight containers and freeze.

"Our favorite when it's too warm for hot meals and you need something filling."

S. Beiler, Woodward, PA

Toasted Oats

12 cups oats
1 cup brown sugar
2 cups butter, melted

4 teaspoons cinnamon
(optional)

Mix all ingredients and bake at 300 degrees for 1 hour, stirring every 20 minutes. Serve as you would cereal with milk or as granola with yogurt.

Anna Weaver, Mertztown, PA

Butterscotch Oatmeal

1 egg, well beaten
2 cups milk
¼ cup brown sugar

¼ teaspoon salt
1 cup oats
2 tablespoons butter

In saucepan, stir together egg, milk, brown sugar, and salt. Add oats. Cook over medium heat until thickened, stirring frequently. Add butter and serve warm.

Mrs. Reuben (Anna) Lapp, Rockville, IN

Baked Oatmeal

3 cups oats
½ cup melted butter
1 teaspoon salt
1 teaspoon cinnamon
1 teaspoon vanilla

2 teaspoons baking powder
1 cup milk
½ to 1 cup brown sugar
2 eggs

Mix all ingredients together and spread into 9x9-inch pan. Bake at 350 degrees for 30 minutes. Optional: top with blueberries, walnuts, pecans, diced apples, or raisins before baking.

Susie King, Allenwood, PA

Breakfast Cereal Cake

8 cups quick oats
4 cups whole wheat flour
3 cups sugar or maple syrup
2 tablespoons baking soda
2 teaspoons salt
4 teaspoons cinnamon

4 teaspoons baking powder
1 cup coconut
1 cup raisins (optional)
1 cup vegetable oil
4 cups milk
2 teaspoons vanilla

Mix oats, flour, sugar, baking soda, salt, cinnamon, and baking powder. Add coconut and raisins. Mix in oil. Add milk and vanilla, mixing well. Divide batter between 2 greased 9x13-inch pans. Bake at 350 degrees for 40 minutes or until done. This is a good whole grain cereal cake that children will like served with milk.

Mrs. Joseph Hochstetler, Danville, OH

OATMEAL PATTIES

To leftover oatmeal add a couple of eggs, a little flour, and salt to taste. Mix well. Drop by spoonful into hot frying pan. Fry until nicely browned on both sides. Serve with maple syrup.

MALINDA GINGERICH, Spartansburg, PA

CORNMEAL MUSH

3 cups water	1 cup cold water
1 cup cornmeal	Salt to taste

In deep saucepan, bring 3 cups water to a boil. Mix cornmeal with 1 cup cold water. Add to boiling water, stirring until thick. Add salt. Simmer for 1½ hours on low heat. Pour into loaf pan and chill. The next morning, slice and fry mush in skillet with oil until golden brown on both sides. Delicious topped with molasses or honey and an egg.

"THE CHICKENS ALSO LOVE LEFTOVERS OF CORNMEAL MUSH."

MRS. JOSEPH SCHWARTZ, Salem, IN

Egg-a-Log

2 cups milk
1 tablespoon flour
Salt to taste

Chicken base to taste
2 hard-boiled eggs, diced
Whole wheat bread

In saucepan, heat milk and add flour, stirring until thickened. Add salt and chicken base. Stir in eggs. Serve over toasted whole wheat bread.

Adel Schmidt, Carlisle, KY

Sausage Gravy

½ pound sausage (can also use leftover sausage)
¼ cup butter

¼ cup flour
Salt and pepper to taste
2½ cups milk

Fry sausage in 2-quart kettle. (Skip the browning part if using leftover sausage.) When browned, add butter and stir until melted. Stir in flour, salt, and pepper. Add milk and stir until thick and bubbly. Serve with mashed potatoes or biscuits. Also good over breakfast pizza.

Miriam Byler, Spartansburg, PA

Best Brunch Enchiladas

2 cups cubed ham	1 tablespoon flour
½ cup chopped green onion	2 cups milk
10 (8 inch) flour tortillas	6 eggs, beaten
2 cups shredded cheddar cheese	¼ teaspoon salt

Combine ham and onion and place about ⅓ cup mixture down the end of each tortilla. Top with about 2 tablespoons cheese. Roll up and place seam down in 9x13-inch baking dish. In bowl, combine flour, milk, eggs, and salt. Pour over tortillas. Cover and refrigerate for 8 hours or overnight. Remove from refrigerator 30 minutes before baking. Cover and bake at 350 degrees for 25 minutes. Uncover and bake for 10 more minutes. Sprinkle with remaining cheese and bake until it melts. Let stand for 10 minutes before serving.

JUDITH MILLER, Fredericktown, OH

Zucchini Frittata

½ cup chopped onion
1 cup shredded zucchini
1 teaspoon oil

3 eggs, beaten
¼ teaspoon salt
1 cup shredded cheese

In oven-safe skillet, sauté onion and zucchini in oil over medium heat for 2 to 3 minutes. Pour eggs over top. Sprinkle with salt. Cook until almost set—6 to 7 minutes. Sprinkle with cheese, then bake at 350 degrees for 5 to 10 minutes until cheese is melted.

Emma Kurtz, Smicksburg, PA

HASH BROWN CHEESE OMELET

1 medium onion
½ cup chopped green pepper
1¾ cups hash brown potatoes
8 eggs

¼ cup water
⅛ teaspoon pepper
2 teaspoons salt
Cheese slices

In large skillet, sauté onion and green pepper. Add potatoes, stirring until heated through. In bowl, beat eggs, water, pepper, and salt. Pour over potatoes. As eggs begin to set, lift edges to let uncooked portion flow underneath. Just before eggs are completely set, place cheese slices over half of the egg and fold omelet in half.

JULIA BEACHY, Salisbury, PA

BREAKFAST PANCAKE PIZZA

Mix your favorite pancake batter. Pour into greased cake pan and bake until done. Then put scrambled eggs on top. Sprinkle with cheese. Make sausage gravy for on top. Eat with or without syrup.

"This is one of our favorites."

AMMON AND EMMA MILLER, Marion Center, PA

Fluffy Pancakes

2 cups flour
2 tablespoons sugar
4 teaspoons baking powder
1 teaspoon salt

2 egg yolks, well beaten
2 cups milk
2 tablespoons butter, melted
2 egg whites, stiffly beaten

In bowl, mix flour, sugar, baking powder, and salt. Add egg yolks, milk, and butter, stirring until combined. Fold in egg whites. Heat frying pan over medium heat. Add some oil. Pour in batter. Watch pancake, and when it becomes bubbly, flip. Cook until golden brown.

Mrs. Kenneth (Irene) Kaufman, West Union, OH

Pancake Mix

4 cups flour
4 cups whole wheat flour
1 cup sugar
2 tablespoons baking soda
2 teaspoons salt

To make pancakes:
2 eggs, well beaten
¼ cup vinegar
2 cups milk
¼ cup vegetable oil
2½ cups pancake mix

Mix all ingredients together and fry on oiled griddle until both sides are browned. Mix all ingredients and store in airtight container.

Susie King, Allenwood, PA

Molasses Pancake Syrup

2 cups molasses
1 cup water
1 cup sugar

1 cup brown sugar
1 teaspoon vanilla

In saucepan, bring molasses, water, sugar, and brown sugar to a boil. Simmer for 5 minutes. Remove from heat and add vanilla.

Susie King, Allenwood, PA

Maple Pancake Syrup

1 cup sugar
2 cups brown sugar
½ cup corn syrup

1 cup water
½ teaspoon maple flavoring
1 tablespoon butter

Combine all ingredients in saucepan and boil for 10 minutes. Serve on pancakes.

Mrs. Kenneth (Irene) Kaufman, West Union, OH

BREADS

And Jesus said unto them, I am the bread of
life: he that cometh to me shall never hunger; and
he that believeth on me shall never thirst.

JOHN 6:35

Bran Muffins

2 cups whole wheat flour
2 teaspoons baking powder
½ teaspoon baking soda
1 teaspoon salt
½ cup brown or raw sugar
1 egg, beaten
½ cup lard or butter
¾ cup sour milk or cream

In bowl, combine whole wheat flour, baking powder, baking soda, salt, and sugar. Work in egg. Add lard and milk, mixing quickly. Pour into muffin tins and bake at 400 to 425 degrees for 20 to 25 minutes. Note: You can add nuts, raisins, dates, or bran. It can be eaten like shortcake with fruit on top or baked like bread.

Mary Kauffman, Albion, PA

Pumpkin Chip Muffins

4 eggs
2 cups sugar
1 (16 ounce) can pumpkin
1½ cups oil
3 cups flour
2 teaspoons baking soda
2 teaspoons baking powder
1 teaspoon cinnamon
1 teaspoon salt
2 cups chocolate chips

In mixing bowl, beat eggs, then beat in sugar, pumpkin, and oil. In another bowl, combine flour, baking soda, baking powder, cinnamon, and salt. Add to pumpkin mixture and mix well. Fold in chocolate chips. Fill greased muffin cups ¾ full. Bake at 400 degrees for 15 to 20 minutes or until done. Cool in pan for 10 minutes before taking out.

Judith Miller, Fredericktown, OH

Lemon Poppy Seed Bread

3 eggs
¼ cup oil
1 cup plain yogurt
1 teaspoon vanilla
3 tablespoons lemon juice

2 tablespoons poppy seeds
2 teaspoons baking powder
½ teaspoon salt
½ cup sugar
2 cups flour

Mix all ingredients together and pour into greased loaf pan. Bake at 350 degrees for approximately 40 minutes. Serve warm with butter and jam.

Nora Miller, Millersburg, OH

Basic Bagel

1½ cups warm water (105 to 115 degrees)

1 ounce package dry yeast

3 tablespoons sugar or 2 tablespoons honey

Approximately 4¼ cups unsifted flour (can use whole wheat for half the flour)

1 teaspoon salt

1 gallon water

Mix warm water, yeast, and sugar. Let sit until bubbly. Stir in flour and salt. Turn onto lightly floured board and knead for 10 minutes, flouring board as needed until dough is smooth and elastic. Cover and let rise in warm place for 15 minutes. Punch down dough and, on lightly floured board, roll into 5x9-inch rectangle 1 inch thick. Cut into 12 strips with floured knife. Roll each strip until ½ inch thick. Moisten ends and join together. Cover and let rise in warm place for 20 minutes.

Bring 1 gallon water to a boil. Lower heat and add 4 bagels. Simmer for exactly 7 minutes. Any longer will cause sogginess. Remove and cool on towel while cooking remaining bagels. Bake on ungreased cookie sheets at 375 degrees for 30 to 35 minutes. Cool and eat, or wrap and freeze. Yield: 1 dozen.

Rebecca Huyard, Coatesville, PA

Best Ever Biscuits

2 cups flour
2 teaspoons sugar
½ teaspoon salt
4 teaspoons baking powder
½ teaspoon cream of tartar
½ cup butter
½ cup milk

In mixing bowl, mix flour, sugar, salt, baking powder, and cream of tartar. Cut in butter until crumbly. Add milk and work until dough comes together. Do not overmix. Roll out and cut 12 biscuits. Bake at 450 degrees for 10 to 12 minutes.

Katie Yoder, Sugarcreek, OH

Honey Wheat Oatmeal Bread

2 cups water
½ cup oats
¼ cup oil
¼ cup honey
2 teaspoons salt
1 tablespoon yeast
1 egg, beaten
1 cup whole wheat flour
White flour

Bring water to a boil and pour over oats. Add oil, honey, and salt. Cool to lukewarm. Add yeast and stir. Then add egg and whole wheat flour. Add enough white flour to make a stiff dough. Dough should be slightly sticky. Knead well. Let rise until doubled in size. Punch down and let rise again. Punch down and separate into 2 loaf pans. Let rise until doubled in size. Bake at 400 degrees for 25 minutes.

Julia Beachy, Salisbury, PA

HEARTY SANDWICH BREAD (GLUTEN-FREE)

2 cups almond flour
1½ to 1¾ cups coconut flour
1 tablespoon baking powder
2 teaspoons salt
2 tablespoons flaxseeds

1 cup warm coconut milk
3 tablespoons coconut oil, melted and cooled
2 tablespoons honey

Mix almond flour, 1½ cups coconut flour, baking powder, salt, and flaxseeds. In another bowl, combine coconut milk, coconut oil, and honey. Add to dry mixture. Add ¼ cup coconut flour if mixture is too loose. Whisk to combine. Scrape dough into 9x5-inch loaf pan greased with coconut oil. Bake at 375 degrees for 20 to 30 minutes until golden brown, rotating pan halfway through baking. Cool for about 15 minutes then flip out onto wire rack to cool to room temperature.

ELIZABETH SWAREY, Charlotte Courthouse, VA

Gluten-Free, Dairy-Free Bread

1¾ cups almond milk or water
2 cups brown rice flour
1¼ cups tapioca flour
1½ tablespoons honey
3½ teaspoons xanthan gum
1 teaspoon salt

4½ teaspoons instant yeast
⅓ cup ground flaxseeds
  or chia seeds
4 eggs, beaten
1 teaspoon vinegar

In saucepan, heat almond milk to 110 degrees. In bowl, mix brown rice flour, tapioca flour, honey, xanthan gum, salt, yeast, and flaxseeds. Add eggs and vinegar to almond milk. Pour over dry mixture and stir to combine. Grease and flour 2 loaf pans. Spoon batter into pans with wet spatula as dough will be wet and sticky. Let rise to pan height. Bake at 350 degrees for 1 hour.

"Our family is gluten and dairy intolerant, so this is our favorite bread recipe."

Mrs. Nathan Delagrange, Vermontville, MI

Breadsticks

1½ cups lukewarm water
1 tablespoon yeast
1 tablespoon sugar
2 tablespoons vegetable oil

1 cup whole wheat flour
Approximately 2¾ cups bread flour
1 teaspoon salt

Mix all ingredients together and spread onto large cookie sheet. Let rise.

Topping:

2 tablespoons grated Parmesan cheese
½ cup Italian dressing or melted butter
1 teaspoon garlic powder

1 tablespoon Italian seasoning
½ tablespoon oregano
Mozzarella cheese
Pepperoni or diced cooked meat (optional)

Mix Parmesan cheese, Italian dressing, garlic powder, Italian seasoning, and oregano together. Pour over risen dough and spread evenly. Bake at 375 degrees for 21 minutes. Remove from oven and sprinkle with mozzarella cheese and pepperoni. Return to oven until cheese melts. Cut bread into strips. Serve dipped in warm pizza sauce or ranch dressing.

RUTH BYLER, Quaker City, OH

Corn Bread

1 teaspoon baking soda	½ cup sugar
1 cup sour milk or buttermilk	1 teaspoon salt
1 cup whole wheat flour	1 egg
1 cup cornmeal	1 tablespoon butter

Dissolve baking soda in milk. In bowl, combine whole wheat flour, cornmeal, sugar, and salt. Mix in egg and butter. Add milk. Pour into greased 9x9-inch pan. Bake at 350 degrees for 30 minutes. Serve with butter and jam along with your favorite soup.

NORA MILLER, Millersburg, OH

Corn Pone

1 cup cornmeal	½ cup whole wheat flour
¼ cup sugar	½ teaspoon salt
½ teaspoon baking soda	1 egg, beaten
1 cup buttermilk	

Mix all ingredients in bowl until well moistened. Pour into greased bread pan. Bake at 350 degrees for 25 to 30 minutes. Serve with maple syrup and milk.

MIRIAM BYLER, Spartansburg, PA

Potato Rolls

1 tablespoon yeast
½ cup warm water
½ cup sugar
½ cup shortening
2 teaspoons salt

1 cup mashed cooked potatoes
3 eggs
1 cup cooking water
 from potatoes
7 to 8 cups flour

In small bowl, dissolve yeast in warm water. In large bowl, cream sugar with shortening. Add salt, then potatoes, eggs, potato water, and yeast mixture. Add enough flour to make a soft, easily handled dough. Let rise for 45 minutes, then divide into approximately 24 balls. Shape into rolls and let rise until doubled in size. Bake at 350 degrees for 20 minutes or until golden brown.

Susie King, Allenwood, PA

Deep-Fried Pizza Dough

1 tablespoon yeast
1 cup warm water
1 teaspoon sugar

1½ teaspoons salt
¼ cup oil
3 cups flour

Mix yeast into warm water. Add sugar, salt, oil, and 1½ cups flour. Beat until there are no more lumps. Gradually add remaining flour. Knead dough for 5 minutes. Roll out ball of dough into circle or square and fill half with pizza ingredients of choice (pepperoni, cheese, etc.). Fold uncovered side of dough over and pinch edges together. Deep-fry. Makes 7 hand-size pizzas.

Martha Miller, Decatur, IN

STICKY BUN SYRUP

1 stick margarine
1 cup brown sugar
2 tablespoons corn syrup

¾ teaspoon cinnamon
Bun or roll dough balls

Mix together margarine, brown sugar, corn syrup, and cinnamon and spread in 2 round cake pans. Put bun dough on top and bake at 350 degrees for 30 minutes. Turn upside down on plate when done. No need for icing.

"I often use this syrup when I'm baking bread or cinnamon rolls. I use the extra bread dough or end pieces cut from cinnamon-roll logs to form dough balls."

EMMA KURTZ, Smicksburg, PA

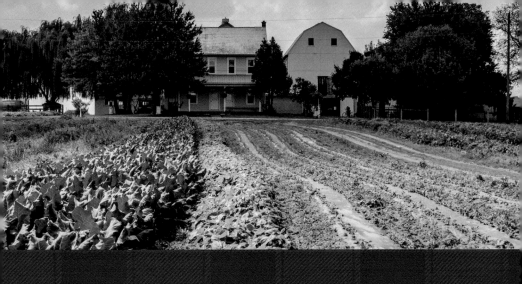

Salads and Side Dishes

*But even the very hairs of your head are
all numbered. Fear not therefore: ye are
of more value than many sparrows.*

LUKE 12:7

DANDELION SALAD

3 cups cut-up dandelion greens
2 cups cubed potatoes, cooked
4 hard-boiled eggs, diced
6 slices bacon, fried

Dressing:
1 cup water
2 tablespoons cornstarch
½ teaspoon salt
2 tablespoons vinegar
¼ cup sugar or stevia
Bacon grease

Mix all dressing ingredients and bring to a boil. Layer greens, potatoes, eggs, and bacon. Top with dressing.

"I prefer to use dandelion greens in early spring."

EMMA BYLER, New Wilmington, PA

Cauliflower and Lettuce Salad

1 head lettuce, finely chopped
1 small head cauliflower,
   finely chopped
1 sweet onion, chopped

1 pound bacon, fried
   and crumbled
2 cups salad dressing
¼ cup sugar
2 cups shredded cheese

In large bowl, mix lettuce, cauliflower, onion, and bacon. Spread salad dressing over top like icing. Sprinkle with sugar and cheese. Let sit in refrigerator overnight. When ready to serve, drain off any water and stir to mix.

Isaac Schwartz, Stanwood, MI

Overnight Salad

1 big head lettuce
1 big head cauliflower
1 pound bacon, fried
   and crumbled

Onion to taste
2 cups mayonnaise
¼ cup sugar
½ cup Parmesan cheese

Layer lettuce, cauliflower, bacon, and onion in big bowl or container. In small bowl, mix mayonnaise, sugar, and cheese. Pour over salad and refrigerate for 24 hours. Stir to mix in dressing just before serving.

Barb Fisher, Ronks, PA

Coleslaw Cabbage

1 head cabbage, shredded, or
   ¾ gallon shredded cabbage
2 cups diced celery
½ cup diced green pepper
2 scant cups sugar

½ cup diluted vinegar
2 tablespoons salt
1½ teaspoons celery seed
1½ teaspoons mustard seed

Place cabbage, celery, and green pepper in large bowl. In small bowl, mix sugar, vinegar, salt, celery seed, and mustard seed well until sugar dissolves. Pour over cabbage and stir well. Refrigerate for 24 hours. Eat fresh, or pack into jars and cold pack for 20 minutes.

Mary Kauffman, Albion, PA

Day B-4 Cabbage Salad

2 cups salad dressing
   or mayonnaise
1½ cups sour cream
1 cup sugar
2 teaspoons salt
8 cups shredded cabbage

1 cup fried and crumbled bacon
½ cup peas
4 cups shredded cheese
2 cups crushed nacho
   tortilla chips
Cherry tomatoes (optional)

In bowl, blend salad dressing, sour cream, sugar, and salt. In large container with lid, layer cabbage, sauce, bacon, peas, and cheese. Chill overnight. Before serving, toss salad to mix well. Top with chips and tomatoes.

Sarah Yoder, Mount Perry, OH

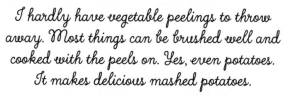
GERMAN SALAD

4 cups cubed cooked potatoes
¾ quart sliced cooked sausage
6 hard-boiled eggs, sliced

¼ pound butter
1 cup flour
Milk

In bowl, combine potatoes, sausage, and eggs. In skillet, melt butter. Stir in flour and cook until lightly browned. Add milk until a nice sauce forms. Pour over potato mixture and stir to coat.

MRS. ALBERT SUMMY, Meyersdale, PA

SAUSAGE SALAD

1 part turkey sausage,
   ham, or chicken

½ part celery
Vegenaise

Use a Tupperware chopper to finely chop the sausage and celery. Then add enough Vegenaise to reach desired consistency.

"My husband really likes this in his lunch. It is very easy to make in a pinch, and I often do it mornings while packing his lunch."

AMANDA KING, Honeybrook, PA

Ham Salad

2 cups chopped potatoes
2 cups macaroni
3½ cups diced ham
3 cups chopped cheese
3 peppers (green, yellow,
  and orange), chopped
Celery, diced

Pepperoni, chopped
8 ounces sour cream
1 cup Miracle Whip dressing
½ cup mustard
14 ounces heavy cream
Sugar to taste
Salt to taste

In saucepan, cook potatoes and macaroni until tender. Drain and cool. Add ham, cheese, peppers, celery, and pepperoni. In bowl, mix sour cream, dressing, mustard, and cream. Season with sugar and salt. Pour over salad mixture and stir to coat. The recipe can easily be adapted to your tastes by adding vegetables and seasonings you prefer.

Malinda Hostetler, West Salem, OH

Baked Beans

2 pounds dried beans (or
  12 cups cooked)
1 small can tomato paste
1 cup ketchup
1 cup brown sugar

2 teaspoons garlic powder
1 pound bacon, hot
  dogs, or sausage
1 onion, chopped

Sort, wash, and drain beans. In large pot of cold water, soak beans for 12 to 24 hours. Drain. Cover with fresh water and cook over low heat for at least 1 hour or in slow cooker for up to 8 hours, until beans are tender (but not mushy). Drain. Add tomato paste, ketchup, brown sugar, and garlic powder. In skillet, brown meat. Add onion and cook until translucent. Add to beans. Pour into large roasting pan. Cover and bake at 350 degrees for 1 to 2 hours.

ALVIN JR. AND RUTH FISHER, Berlin, PA

Navy Beans

4 cups cooked navy
  beans, drained
1 cup heavy cream
2 pats butter
5 slices cheese
½ cup ketchup

½ cup brown sugar
2 teaspoons mustard
Chopped onion
Salt and pepper to taste
Chopped ham, hot
  dogs, or bacon

Combine all ingredients in pot over medium heat and cook until hot.

ARLENE BONTREGER, Middlebury, IN

GREEN BEANS

3 tablespoons butter	1 quart hot, drained green beans
3 tablespoons flour	3 hard-boiled eggs, sliced
2 cups milk	3 slices toasted bread, cubed
¼ pound cheese, sliced	

In saucepan, melt butter. Add flour and stir to cook a bit. Add milk and cook until thickened. Add cheese, keeping 6 to 8 slices for later, and stir to melt. Place beans in casserole dish. Cover with cheese sauce. Dot with slices of egg. Top with bread cubes. Cover with reserved cheese slices. Bake at 350 degrees for 15 minutes, or just long enough to melt cheese.

"I like to use fresh or frozen green beans in this."

JULIA BEACHY, Salisbury, PA

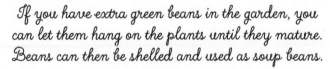

TIP:

If you have extra green beans in the garden, you can let them hang on the plants until they mature. Beans can then be shelled and used as soup beans.

MRS. BETHANY MARTIN, Homer City, PA

THREE-WAY BEETS

My husband and I both enjoy eating the beets we grow in our garden every year, and we like to use them in three different ways. The first thing we do once the beets have been brought in from the garden is to wash them well. Following that, we cut off the greens that are close to the top of the beets. The beets themselves are reserved for another meal. Here is my recipe for the beet greens:

SIMPLE BEET GREENS

Put beet greens in a steamer basket that has been placed inside kettle filled with enough water to boil, but do not cover greens with water. Put lid on kettle and turn burner on high. Once water starts to boil, heat is turned to medium-low and beet greens are allowed to steam until they are tender (2 to 5 minutes). When they are done, remove steamer basket and transfer greens to serving dish. Then add a pat of butter and salt and pepper to taste. The beet greens will accompany whatever meat dish or other vegetables you may choose to fix.

TASTY BOILED BEETS

So that peeling beets is easier, precook whole beets for 20 minutes or until they feel soft. Pour and strain juice into jar or separate container, cool, and refrigerate. Cool beets enough so that you can handle them, and then holding each beet firmly, twist your hands in opposite directions. Skin should slide right off. Let beets cool more before slicing them. Place beets in kettle and cover with water. Cook on medium until beets are heated and cooked well. Before serving, add a few pats of butter and salt and pepper to taste.

HEALTHY BEET JUICE

Beet juice stored in refrigerator can be consumed either cold or warm. My husband prefers to drink his cold. One to two cups per day is enough to give a person the following health benefits: helps to lower blood pressure; helps with circulation; is a liver support; reduces cholesterol; offers energy and stamina; is a good source of potassium and other minerals.

Note: anyone prone to calcium oxalate kidney stones should avoid drinking too much beet juice, as it is high in oxalates.

WANDA E. BRUNSTETTER

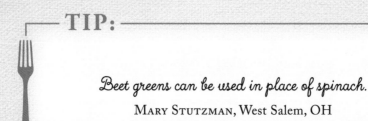

CORN

For too-old sweet corn, those with such large kernels: Use grater and make creamed corn. Do this while corn is still raw by rubbing corn up and down over the larger holes on grater. Some kernels will stay on the cob, but the milk and pulp will squeeze out.

After you cut raw sweet corn off the cob, take a knife and scrape the cob. The pulp makes delicious corn fritters or creamed corn. The pulp can easily be frozen in small containers for later use. (Creamed corn, though, can spoil easily when canned.)

MRS. BETHANY MARTIN, Homer City, PA

HONEY-GLAZED CARROTS

1 pound baby carrots
Salt to taste
2 tablespoons butter
2 tablespoons honey

1 tablespoon lemon juice
Salt and pepper to taste
¼ cup chopped parsley

In medium saucepan, bring some water to a boil. Add carrots and salt; cook for 5 to 6 minutes until tender. Drain. Add butter, honey, and lemon juice. Cook until glaze coats carrots, about 5 minutes. Season with salt and pepper. Garnish with parsley.

KATIE ZOOK, Apple Creek, OH

Cauliflower Cheese Casserole

1 head or about 1½
   pounds cauliflower
1 small red pepper, chopped
1 small green pepper, chopped
1 clove garlic, minced
1 tablespoon butter
2 tablespoons cornstarch
1½ cups milk

2 tablespoons butter
1 teaspoon salt
¼ teaspoon pepper
1 cup shredded cheese
2 tablespoons fine dry
   breadcrumbs
1 tablespoon melted butter

Separate cauliflower into florets. Drop into boiling salted water and cook for 5 minutes. Drain then arrange in 2-quart buttered baking dish. In skillet, sauté red pepper, green pepper, and garlic in 1 tablespoon butter. When done, sprinkle over cauliflower. In bowl, mix cornstarch with milk. To skillet, add 2 tablespoons butter and melt. Stir in milk mixture and cook, stirring until thickened. Add salt, pepper, and cheese, stirring until cheese melts. Pour over cauliflower. In bowl, mix breadcrumbs with melted butter and sprinkle on top. Bake at 350 degrees for 25 minutes.

RUTH YODER, Berlin, PA

Baked Mushroom Rice

½ cup rice (not instant)
1⅓ cups chicken broth
1 cup sliced mushroom
    pieces, fresh or canned
1 medium onion, chopped

¼ teaspoon dried basil
¼ teaspoon dried oregano
⅛ teaspoon lemon
    pepper (optional)
Salt to taste

Combine all ingredients in 1½-quart casserole dish coated with nonstick cooking spray. Cover and bake at 350 degrees for 45 minutes or until rice is tender.

Anna Weaver, Mertztown, PA

Hot Water Noodles

3¾ cups egg yolks
1½ tablespoons salt

1½ cups boiling water
16 cups pastry flour

Put egg yolks and salt in bowl and stir until deep orange in color. Stir in boiling water and add flour all at once. Knead until smooth and well mixed. Put through noodle cutter and spread out to dry.

Isaac Schwartz, Stanwood, MI

POTATO FILLING

Onion, chopped
Celery, chopped
2 tablespoons butter
2 eggs
1 cup milk

½ teaspoon celery salt (optional)
¼ teaspoon seasoned salt
4 slices bread
1 cup mashed potatoes

In skillet, sauté desired amount of onion and celery in butter until soft. In bowl, beat eggs and milk together. Stir in onion, celery, celery salt, and seasoned salt. Pour over crumbled bread. Mix well. Stir in potatoes. Spread in casserole dish, cover, and bake at 350 degrees for 1 hour or at 150 degrees for all afternoon. Also good with meat and/or peas added.

"A good way to use that little bit of leftover mashed potatoes, along with bread heels that don't get eaten."

ANNA WEAVER, Mertztown, PA

39965102768479

LEFTOVER MASHED POTATOES

2 cups mashed potatoes
3 cups diced ham or bologna
1 cup shredded cheese
½ cup salad dressing
   or mayonnaise
¼ cup minced onion
1 teaspoon mustard
½ teaspoon pepper
3½ cups cornflakes, crushed

Mix potatoes, ham, cheese, salad dressing, onion, mustard, and pepper. Roll mixture into balls then roll into crushed cornflakes. Bake on cookie sheet at 350 degrees for 30 minutes.

FANNIE MILLER, Pierpont, OH

CREAMY BAKED POTATO CASSEROLE

Grate as many potatoes as you need for your meal. Add salt and pepper to taste. You can also add onion, cabbage, peppers, or meat of your choice. Pour heavy cream over to cover everything. Bake until done. Then top with cheese.

AMANDA SWARTZENTRUBER, Dalton, OH

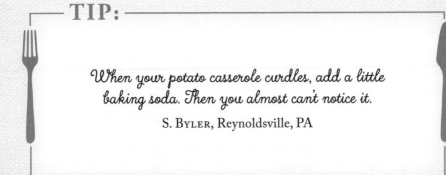

TIP:

When your potato casserole curdles, add a little baking soda. Then you almost can't notice it.

S. BYLER, Reynoldsville, PA

Potato Puffs

1 cup mashed potatoes
1 to 2 eggs, beaten
¼ teaspoon salt

¼ to ½ cup flour
1 teaspoon baking powder

Mix all ingredients well. Fry teaspoonfuls in lard or butter in frying pan.

Isaac Schwartz, Stanwood, MI
Mrs. Chester Miller, Centerville, PA

"Can top with a slice of cheese, if desired."
Grace Ann Miller, Big Prairie, OH

Hash Browns

3 cups finely shredded potatoes
2 eggs, well beaten

1½ teaspoons baking powder
½ to 1 teaspoon salt

In mixing bowl, gently combine potatoes and eggs. Combine baking powder and salt before mixing into potatoes. Drop by tablespoonful into hot oil. Brown lightly on both sides.

Ammon and Emma Miller, Marion Center, PA

Potato Wedges

6 medium potatoes
1 teaspoon paprika
½ teaspoon salt
2 teaspoons seasoned salt
½ teaspoon pepper
½ teaspoon baking powder

1 cup flour
2 teaspoons sour cream
and onion powder
2 teaspoons cheese powder
2 teaspoons chicken seasoning
½ cup margarine

Wash and cut up potatoes in long wedges, not too thin. Put paprika, salt, seasoned salt, pepper, baking powder, flour, sour cream and onion powder, cheese powder, and chicken seasoning in bowl and mix. Roll potato wedges in mixture. Melt margarine and pour half in bottom of cookie sheet. Spread potatoes on top and drizzle with remaining butter. Bake at 400 degrees for 45 minutes, turning potatoes halfway through.

David and Martha Yoder, Grantsville, MD

FRENCH FRIES

Potatoes
Coconut oil
Salt

Peel the amount of potatoes you need per person. Cut into fries. Melt enough coconut oil to just coat potatoes (maybe 1 tablespoon to 4 potatoes). Oil a baking sheet. Place fries in single layer on pan. Bake at 425 degrees for 45 to 55 minutes, stirring every 10 minutes. Sprinkle with salt as soon as done.

"These are just as good as deep-fried fries and take almost no oil."

RACHEL MILLER, Millersburg, OH

GLAZED SWEET POTATOES

6 to 8 sweet potatoes, cut
   into 1½-inch chunks
   and lightly cooked
¼ cup brown sugar

¼ cup maple syrup
¼ cup butter
¼ teaspoon cinnamon
¼ teaspoon salt

Place sweet potatoes in 2-quart baking dish. In small saucepan, bring brown sugar, maple syrup, butter, cinnamon, and salt to a boil. Pour over sweet potatoes and bake at 350 degrees for 30 minutes or until tender and hot.

SADIE FISHER, Aaronsburg, PA

Squash Medley

½ medium green zucchini, sliced or chunked

½ medium gold zucchini, sliced or chunked

2 to 4 pods okra, sliced

½ small onion, chopped

¼ large green pepper, chopped

16 ounces canned tomatoes or 3 fresh tomatoes, chopped

1 chicken bouillon cube

½ teaspoon minced garlic

1 teaspoon sugar

½ teaspoon salt

Place all ingredients in saucepan. Bring to a boil; lower heat. Let simmer until vegetables are tender.

Spaghetti Squash

To cook a spaghetti squash, cut it in half lengthwise. Scoop out seeds. Place cut sides down in baking pan and add water to cover bottom of pan ½ inch deep. Bake at 350 degrees for 45 minutes or until tender.

Serving suggestions:

1 – Brown butter and pour into baked halves.

2 – Heat spaghetti sauce and pour desired amount into baked halves.

3 – When slightly cooled to handle, scoop squash out of shell and shred with fork. Serve with spaghetti sauce, meatballs, and grated parmesan cheese.

Anna Weaver, Mertztown, PA

Tomato Casserole

Fresh tomatoes
Green peppers, sliced in rings
Onion, sliced in rings
Sugar
Salt

Pepper
Butter
Breadcrumbs or
   crushed crackers

Peel tomatoes if you wish. Slice tomatoes and place in 9x13-inch pan. Arrange pepper and onion rings over tomatoes. Season to taste with sugar, salt, and pepper. Melt butter and mix with breadcrumbs. Cover vegetables with crumbs. Bake at 350 degrees for 1 to 1½ hours.

"A different twist on plain veggies. Even my children who generally don't eat onions and peppers love this."

Anna Weaver, Mertztown, PA

Stewed Tomatoes

1 quart canned tomatoes	2 tablespoons flour
1 teaspoon salt	½ cup milk
¼ cup sugar	Saltine crackers or bread
1 tablespoon butter	

In medium saucepan, cook tomatoes with salt for 15 minutes. Add sugar and butter. In bowl, slowly combine flour and milk until no lumps remain. Add floury milk to tomatoes, stirring over heat until thickened. To serve, break up crackers or bread in serving dish and pour tomatoes over them. Stir and serve.

Vegetable Mix

Chopped vegetables
  (butternut squash, sweet
  potatoes, onions, carrots,
  kohlrabi, cabbage,
  cauliflower, turnips, etc.)

Salt and pepper to taste
Sliced apple

Steam vegetables in pan with a little water. Season with salt and pepper. Keep lid on. When about ¾ way cooked, add apple slices. Cover and cook until tender.

Arlene Bontreger, Middlebury, IN

String Bean Patties

1 quart canned green beans
2 eggs
1½ cups quick oats

½ sleeve saltine
  crackers, crushed
½ teaspoon seasoned salt
Flour

Mash beans until very fine. Mix in eggs, oats, crackers, and seasoned salt. Form into patties. Roll in flour to coat. Fry until browned and crisp on both sides. Serve like a hamburger sandwich with lettuce, cheese, and onion.

"Very good for when the supply of meat is running low."

Rachel Miller, Millersburg, OH

Onion Patties

2½ cups chopped onion
1 tablespoon sugar
1 teaspoon salt

1 tablespoon cornmeal
¾ cup flour
Milk

Mix onion, sugar, salt, cornmeal, and flour. Add just enough milk to make a thick batter. Drop by spoonful onto hot buttered skillet. Fry each side until golden brown.

Malinda Gingerich, Spartansburg, PA

Potato Cakes

1½ cups mashed potatoes
2 eggs
4 tablespoons flour

Mix all together until no lumps remain. Drop by tablespoonful onto hot oiled griddle and fry until golden on both sides. Serve with gravy for breakfast or lunch.

John Llyod and Susan Yoder, Newaygo, MI

Potato Pancakes

2 cups grated potatoes
1 tablespoon minced onion
1 teaspoon salt
1 egg, beaten
2 tablespoons butter

4 tablespoons flour
1 teaspoon baking powder
¼ teaspoon pepper
2 tablespoons milk

Mix all ingredients well and drop by spoonful onto hot buttered skillet. Fry both sides until brown and crisp.

Malinda Gingerich, Spartansburg, PA

Garden Fish (Fried Zucchini)

Zucchini
Breadcrumbs
Flour

Salt and pepper to taste
Bacon grease

Slice zucchini into circles or oblong slices. Combine breadcrumbs and flour. Season with salt and pepper. Roll zucchini in mixture then fry in bacon grease until tender-soft. Makes a tasty side dish.

MRS. CHESTER MILLER, Centerville, PA

Zucchini-Cheese Patties

1 cup grated zucchini
1 small onion, chopped
½ cup shredded cheddar cheese

2 eggs
Salt and pepper to taste
Cracker or bread crumbs

Mix zucchini, onion, cheese, and eggs. Season with salt and pepper. Add enough cracker crumbs to form patties. Fry in oil for 2 to 3 minutes on each side until browned.

MALINDA GINGERICH, Spartansburg, PA

Zucchini Patties

2 cups grated zucchini
1 teaspoon salt
2 tablespoons sugar

½ cup flour
2 tablespoons minced onion

Mix all ingredients together. Drop by spoonful onto hot greased skillet. Fry each side until golden brown.

MALINDA GINGERICH, Spartansburg, PA

Old-Fashioned Skillet Gravy

After you are done frying meat, add 2 tablespoons flour to the skillet you used and fry until browned. Stir constantly so it won't scorch. Slowly add hot water, stirring constantly until desired thickness. Season with salt and pepper.

"Nothing is wasted!"

John Llyod and Susan Yoder, Newaygo, MI

Delicious Pan Gravy

¼ cup bacon grease
⅓ cup flour

3 to 4 cups milk
Salt to taste

In skillet, heat bacon grease and stir in flour until very brown. Slowly add milk, stirring constantly so you have no lumps. When gravy is at desired thickness, remove from heat and add salt. You can add more or less grease and flour to meet your needs. Measurements are approximate.

"I save all my bacon grease and use it to fry eggs, potatoes, meats, etc. It can also be used to pop popcorn. If I have grease with lots of bacon bits in it, I scrape it into a separate jar and use it to make this gravy."

Mrs. Chester Miller, Centerville, PA

Main Dishes

"A house is built by human hands, but
a home is built by human hearts."

RHODA MILLER, DECATUR, IN

Anything Casserole

Leftover vegetables
Leftover potatoes

Leftover meat
Cheese or leftover gravy

Layer vegetables, potatoes, and meat in casserole dish. Cover with cheese or gravy. Bake at 350 degrees for 30 minutes to warm through.

Mrs. Nathan Delagrange, Vermontville, MI

Shepherd's Pie

Leftover mashed potatoes
Leftover cooked vegetables
Leftover meat, cubed

Breadcrumbs
Leftover gravy

Line greased casserole dish with mashed potatoes. Cover with vegetables and meat. Top with breadcrumbs, then pour gravy over all. Bake at 350 degrees for 40 minutes.

Note: If you have no gravy, beat 1 egg and add 1 cup milk. Season with salt and pepper. Then layer meat and vegetables in casserole dish. Pour egg mixture over. Top with mashed potatoes, and skip the breadcrumbs. Cheese sprinkled on top or browned butter is good to add before serving.

Esther L. Miller, Fredericktown, OH

CORN BREAD CASSEROLE

1 quart canned pork, beef,
   or chicken chunks
Cornstarch
16 ounces mixed
   vegetables, drained

Salt and pepper to taste
Garlic powder to taste
Nutmeg to taste
1 batch corn bread batter

In 2- or 3-quart kettle, place meat and fill ¾ full of water. Thicken with a little cornstarch, but not too thick. Add vegetables and season with salt, pepper, garlic powder, and nutmeg. Cook until hot and thickened. Pour into 9x13-inch pan. Mix your favorite corn bread batter and drop by tablespoonful onto hot gravy. Bake at 350 degrees for 20 to 30 minutes or until corn bread is done.

"Very good. This can be adapted to use fresh meat and vegetables that you have on hand for an inexpensive, filling meal."

Mrs. Matthew C. Girod, Berne, IN

"Something Else Again" Casserole

1 pound ground beef
1 medium onion, chopped
1 teaspoon garlic salt
16 ounces green beans
  or peas, drained
2½ cups cooked rice
1 can cream of mushroom soup

¾ cup sour cream or
  mayonnaise
Dash milk (optional)
Velveeta cheese, sliced
2 cups crushed cornflakes
  or Ritz crackers
¼ cup melted butter

In skillet, brown beef and onion. Add garlic salt, green beans, rice, soup, and sour cream. You can add a bit of milk if it seems dry. Put in casserole dish and cover with cheese slices. In bowl, mix cornflakes and butter. Sprinkle over cheese. Bake at 350 degrees for 30 minutes or until heated through and cheese is melted. Surprisingly good and definitely different! Try it with toppings like salsa, lettuce, sour cream, ranch dressing, nacho chips, etc.

Sarah Byler, Emienton, PA

Stove-Top Potato Meal

Sliced potatoes
2 quarts canned green beans
Leftover meat

Mushrooms (optional)
Cheese (optional)
Leftover gravy (optional)

In large skillet, fry potatoes in oil until tender-crisp. Top with green beans and meat. Add mushrooms. Top with cheese or gravy. Let simmer to heat through.

"A favorite fast, cheap meal for unexpected company."

Mrs. Nathan Delagrange, Vermontville, MI

Katie's Casserole

3 cups uncooked noodles
3 cups ripple-cut potatoes

2 cups cooked meat
Cheese or breadcrumbs

In casserole dish, combine noodles and potatoes. Cover with water. Spread meat over. Top with your choice of cheese or breadcrumbs. Cover and bake at 350 degrees for 1 hour until potatoes and noodles are tender. Can uncover the last 10 minutes to brown the top.

Lydianne K. Hertzler, Charlotte Courthouse, VA

Cowboy Casserole

4 cups cooked and
  sliced potatoes
1 pound ground beef, browned

1 onion, sliced
2 cans pork and beans
Cheese

Mix potatoes, beef, onion, and beans in casserole dish and top with cheese. Bake at 350 degrees for 30 minutes or until hot and bubbly.

Henry D. Byler, New Castle, PA

Chicken Combo

9 slices bread, cubed
4 cups chopped cooked chicken
¼ cup melted butter
½ cup mayonnaise
4 eggs

1 cup milk
1 cup chicken broth
9 slices cheese
2 cans cream of chicken soup

Put bread in bottom of large greased casserole dish. Put chicken on top. In bowl, mix butter, mayonnaise, eggs, milk, and broth. Pour over chicken. Top with cheese. Spread soup over cheese. Prepare topping and spread over soup. Bake at 350 degrees for 1¼ hours.

TOPPING:
1 stick butter
1½ sleeves Ritz crackers, crushed

Mix butter and cracker crumbs.

RACHEL BEILER, Leola, PA

Chicken Vegetable Casserole

1 bag frozen mixed vegetables
    or 2 cans, drained
2 pounds chicken,
    cooked and cubed

2 cans cream of chicken soup
2 cups crushed cornflakes
¼ cup melted butter

Mix vegetables, chicken, and soup and put in casserole dish. Bake at 350 degrees for 50 minutes. In bowl, mix cornflakes and butter. Spread over casserole and bake for 10 more minutes.

AMELIA STUTZMAN, Apple Creek, OH

Cheeseburger Bacon Pasta

8 ounces tube or spiral pasta
½ to 1 pound ground beef
1 can condensed tomato soup
6 strips bacon, fried
   and crumbled

1 cup shredded cheddar cheese
Barbecue sauce
Mustard

In pot, cook pasta. Drain. In skillet, brown beef. Mix in soup. Add pasta and bacon. Heat through. Sprinkle with cheese. Cover and heat until cheese is melted. Serve with barbecue sauce and mustard.

Mrs. Reuben N. Byler, Dayton, PA

HAMBURGER POTATO CASSEROLE

2 pounds ground beef
1 medium onion, chopped
¼ teaspoon pepper
1 teaspoon salt
2 cups macaroni or pasta shells
16 ounces pizza sauce

8 cups cubed potatoes
3 cups milk
1 teaspoon salt
2 rounded tablespoons flour
1 pound Velveeta cheese

In skillet, fry beef with onion and season with pepper and salt. Pour into roast pan or 2 casserole dishes. In pot of water, cook macaroni until tender; drain. Add pizza sauce to macaroni and spread over beef. In pot of water, cook potatoes until tender; drain. Add milk, salt, and flour to potatoes, mixing well. Add cheese and mix. Pour over macaroni. Bake at 350 degrees for 45 to 60 minutes until hot and bubbly throughout.

ESTHER COBLENTZ, Fredericksburg, OH

Potluck Taco Casserole

2 pounds ground beef
2 envelopes taco seasoning
4 large eggs
¾ cup milk
1¼ cups biscuit or baking mix
⅛ teaspoon pepper

½ cup sour cream
2 to 3 cups chopped lettuce
¾ cup chopped tomatoes
2 green onions, chopped
¼ cup chopped green pepper
2 cups shredded cheese

In large skillet, cook beef over medium heat for 10 to 12 minutes or until no longer pink, stirring to break into crumbles. Drain. Add taco seasoning. Spread beef into bottom of 9x13-inch baking dish. In large bowl, beat eggs and milk. Stir in biscuit mix and pepper. Pour over beef. Bake at 400 degrees, uncovered, for 20 to 25 minutes or until golden brown. Cool for 5 to 10 minutes. Spread sour cream over top. Sprinkle with lettuce, tomatoes, onions, green pepper, and cheese.

ALVIN JR. AND RUTH FISHER, Berlin, PA

Deep-Dish Taco Squares

2 cups flour
4 teaspoons baking powder
½ teaspoon cream of tartar
½ teaspoon salt
½ cup lard
1 egg
⅔ cup milk
1 pound ground beef

3 cups whole canned
  tomatoes, drained
½ cup chopped green pepper
2 cups cooked black
  beans, drained
1 cup sour cream
⅔ cup salad dressing
2 tablespoons chopped onion
1 cup shredded cheese

In mixing bowl, combine flour, baking powder, cream of tartar, and salt. Cut in lard and egg. Mix in milk. Spread in greased glass casserole dish. In skillet, brown beef. Add tomatoes, peppers, and beans. Spread over first layer. In bowl, mix sour cream, salad dressing, onion, and cheese. Spread over meat mixture. Bake at 325 degrees for 30 minutes or until hot throughout.

ARLENE BONTREGER, Middlebury, IN

Spanish Rice

1 cup rice	1 teaspoon salt
1 pound ground beef	Dash pepper
1 onion, chopped	3 cups tomato juice

Cook rice until tender. Brown beef in skillet with onion. Add salt and pepper to beef. Add tomato juice and rice. Simmer until juice is reduced.

Mrs. Albert Summy, Meyersdale, PA

Winter Vegetable Casserole

1 to 2 winter squash (e.g., butternut or spaghetti squash)	3 to 4 carrots, sliced
1 small head cabbage	Salt and pepper to taste
1 to 2 quarts green beans	Sour cream
Sliced onion	Cheese (optional)

Wash, peel, and cut squash into chunks. Put in bottom of roasting pan or large casserole dish. Cut cabbage into small pieces and place over squash. Drain beans and place on top. Cover with onion and carrots. Sprinkle with salt and pepper (add other seasonings if desired). Cover with sour cream and cheese. Bake at 350 degrees for 45 to 60 minutes until vegetables are soft.

Katie Petersheim, Lakeview, MI

Pizza Casserole

1 to 2 pounds ground beef
½ green pepper, chopped
1 can cream of mushroom soup
16 ounces pizza sauce
1 can mushroom pieces
   with liquid

¼ teaspoon garlic salt
½ teaspoon oregano
½ cup Parmesan cheese
1 (8 ounce) package noodles
Pepperoni
Mozzarella cheese

In skillet, fry beef until browned. Add green pepper, soup, pizza sauce, mushrooms, garlic salt, oregano, Parmesan cheese, and noodles. Mix and put into casserole dish. Top with pepperoni and mozzarella cheese. Let this sit several hours to overnight before baking at 350 degrees for 1 hour.

Judith Miller, Fredericktown, OH

Pizza Rice Casserole

1 cup rice
2½ cups water
1 teaspoon salt
Sour cream or mayonnaise
Pizza sauce
Meat (sausage, ham,
  bacon, etc.)
Mushrooms

Onion (optional)
Green pepper (optional)
Pepperoni
Tomatoes, fresh and chopped
Banana or hot peppers
  (optional)
Shredded cheese

In saucepan, combine rice, water, and salt and boil until rice is soft and water is absorbed—20 to 30 minutes on low heat. Put rice in bottom of 8x8-inch cake pan. Add in layers sour cream, pizza sauce, meat, mushrooms, onion, green pepper, pepperoni, tomatoes, banana peppers, and cheese. Bake at 350 degrees for 30 minutes or until bubbly at edges. Note: Be sure to use plenty of pizza sauce as it gets dry during baking. Use your imagination for toppings.

"My mom came up with this, and we really like it."

Sarah Byler, Emienton, PA

Rice Pizza Crust

1 cup cooked rice
1 egg
½ cup shredded cheese

½ cup salsa
2 tablespoons melted butter
½ teaspoon salt

Mix all ingredients together and pat thin onto baking sheet. Bake at 350 degrees for 10 to 15 minutes. Add toppings as desired.

Katie Ann Fisher, Christiana, PA

Zucchini Skillet Supper

1 medium zucchini
½ stick butter
1 medium tomato, diced
1 small onion, diced
Leftover meat (sausage,
    hamburger, or other)
1 (8 ounce) can
    mushrooms, drained
16 ounces salsa
16 ounces sour cream
Seasoned salt to taste
2 cups shredded cheese

Peel and grate zucchini. Heat large skillet; add butter. After butter is melted, add zucchini, tomato, onion, meat, and mushrooms. Stir well. Add salsa and sour cream, mixing well. Season with seasoned salt. Stir periodically until thoroughly hot. Top with shredded cheese.

"This is a great recipe for when the garden is in full swing and you don't know what to do with all your zucchini. Also a nice way to use leftover meat."

EllaMae Hilty, Berne, IN

Zucchini Casserole

3 cups grated zucchini
1 cup Bisquick
½ pound sausage or
    ground beef, browned
½ cup chopped onion
½ cup grated cheese
¼ teaspoon salt
Pepper to taste
2 tablespoons parsley
½ cup vegetable oil
4 eggs, beaten
½ teaspoon oregano
½ teaspoon seasoned salt

Mix all ingredients together and put in casserole dish. Bake at 350 degrees for 30 minutes.

Anna Weaver, Mertztown, PA

BBQ Chicken Sandwiches

½ cup chopped onion
½ cup diced celery
1 clove garlic, mined
1 tablespoon butter
½ cup salsa
½ cup ketchup
2 tablespoons brown sugar
2 tablespoons apple
  cider vinegar

1 tablespoon
  Worcestershire sauce
½ teaspoon chili powder
¼ teaspoon salt
⅛ teaspoon pepper
2 cups shredded cooked chicken
6 hamburger buns,
  split and toasted

In saucepan, sauté onion, celery, and garlic in butter until tender. Stir in salsa, ketchup, brown sugar, vinegar, Worcestershire sauce, chili powder, salt, and pepper. Add chicken and stir to coat. Bring to a boil. Reduce heat, cover, and simmer for 15 minutes. Serve about ⅓ cup hot mixture on each bun.

RUTH YODER, Berlin, PA

Chicken Burgers

2 pounds ground chicken
1½ cups finely crushed
  saltine crackers
2 teaspoons chicken base
1 teaspoon seasoned salt

¼ teaspoon pepper
¾ cup milk
1½ teaspoons salt
2 tablespoons brown sugar

Mix all ingredients until well combined. Form into approximately 8 patties. Fry in oil over medium heat for 5 minutes on each side.

ELIZABETH SHROCK, Jamestown, PA

Mock Hamburgers

Here is a recipe for when you don't have plenty of meat.

1 cup chopped cooked
    chicken, tuna, or canned
    green beans, drained
½ sleeve saltine
    crackers, crushed

1 egg
Salt and pepper to taste
Milk (optional)

Stir together chicken, crackers, and egg. Season with salt and pepper. If too dry to form a patty, add just a dash of milk. Fry patties in vegetable oil until browned on both sides.

"We like it with dressings like Miracle Whip, tartar sauce, or Thousand Island dressing. Goes well with a side of noodles or potatoes and a salad for a hearty meal."

Sarah Byler, Emienton, PA

Cheeseburger Subs

2 pounds ground beef
¼ cup chopped onion
10 slices American cheese
1 can cream of mushroom soup
4 ounces cream cheese

1 teaspoon oregano
Toppings (mayonnaise,
    lettuce, sliced onion,
    sliced tomatoes, etc.)

In skillet, fry beef and onion until browned. Drain. Add cheese, soup, cream cheese, and oregano. Mix well and cook until cheese is melted. Serve hot on rolls with toppings.

Mrs. Reuben N. Byler, Dayton, PA

Cheese Topping for Burgers

1 cup shredded cheese
⅓ cup mushrooms
¼ cup mayonnaise

6 slices bacon, fried
    and crumbled

Mix all ingredients and refrigerate. When grilling burgers, spoon ¼ cup mixture over each burger when almost done.

Katie Zook, Apple Creek, OH

GRILLED HAMBURGERS

2 pounds ground beef
2 eggs
1 cup breadcrumbs or quick oats
1 teaspoon onion powder
1 teaspoon garlic powder

1 teaspoon seasoned salt
½ teaspoon pepper
½ cup milk or cream
1 small onion, finely diced

Mix all ingredients together well. Form into patties. Grill over hot coals for 5 to 7 minutes. Flip hamburgers and grill for an additional 5 to 7 minutes until done.

Mrs. Reuben (Anna) Lapp, Rockville, IN

BURGERS

2 pounds ground beef
1½ cups oats
1 cup milk
¼ cup ketchup
4 to 5 teaspoons Meadowcreek
  seasoning or salt and pepper

3 teaspoons Worcestershire
  sauce
2 teaspoons liquid smoke
½ cup brown sugar or
  other sweetener

Mix all ingredients well and form into patties. Fry or grill. Very good grilled over a campfire.

REBECCA STOLTZFUS, Hagerstown, IN

SLOPPY JOE SANDWICHES

2½ pounds ground beef
1 medium onion, chopped
2½ tablespoons
  Worcestershire sauce

1 can cream of mushroom soup
⅓ cup brown sugar
½ cup ketchup
1 tablespoon mustard

In large skillet, fry beef and onion until done. Add Worcestershire sauce, soup, brown sugar, ketchup, and mustard. Mix well and cook until thickened. Serve on bread or buns.

ELIZABETH MILLER, Millersburg, OH

Baked Country Ham

1 country ham
1 cup vinegar
1 cup dark brown sugar
3 whole cloves

1¼ cups dry mustard
1½ cups dark brown sugar
2 tablespoons cornmeal

Day 1: In large roaster or stockpot, soak ham overnight in enough cold water to cover it.

Day 2: In the morning, remove ham from water and place in sink. Scrub with brush to remove any debris. Wash roaster or stockpot and return ham to it. Cover with water. Add vinegar and 1 cup dark brown sugar. Bring to a boil, then immediately reduce heat to low. Simmer for 20 minutes per pound for older ham or 15 to 18 minutes per pound for quick-aged ham—or until the small bone in the hock can be pulled out with your fingers. Let cool in cooking water overnight.

Day 3: Remove cooked ham from liquid and place on rack to drain. Trim fat to about ½ inch thick, score, and stud with cloves. In bowl, mix dry mustard, 1½ cups dark brown sugar, and cornmeal. Apply mixture uniformly over ham. Place ham in open baking pan with rack. Bake at 375 degrees for 20 to 30 minutes or until evenly browned. Remove from oven and cool on rack. Refrigerate overnight.

Day 4: Slice paper thin and serve.

ESTHER L. MILLER, Fredericktown, OH

Barbecued Ham

1 cup ketchup
¼ cup butter
2 tablespoons brown sugar
2 teaspoons mustard
2 tablespoons vinegar

1 cup chopped onion
½ cup water (optional)
1 pound cubed or chipped
  ham or hot dogs

Mix ketchup, butter, brown sugar, mustard, vinegar, onion, and water. Pour over ham and mix to coat. Cook in large skillet on stove, stirring often, or bake at 350 degrees, uncovered, until heated through.

ALVIN JR. AND RUTH FISHER, Berlin, PA

BBQ Chuck Roast

Salt and pepper a chuck roast on both sides, then brown on both sides in skillet. Place in pressure cooker with 2 inches water. Cook under 10 pounds pressure for 1 hour. Let cooker cool down slowly. Remove meat and pull apart. Add ketchup, barbecue sauce, vinegar, mustard, and brown sugar to your taste. Use the water from cooking as broth to thin sauce.

Arlene Bontreger, Middlebury, IN

COUNTRY FRIED STEAK

½ cup flour
½ teaspoon salt
½ teaspoon pepper
¾ cup buttermilk
4 cube steaks

1 cup crushed saltine crackers
3 tablespoons oil
1 can cream of mushroom soup
1 cup milk

In plastic bag or bowl, combine flour, salt, and pepper. Place buttermilk in shallow bowl. Coat steaks with flour mixture then dip into buttermilk and coat with cracker crumbs. In large skillet over medium-high heat, cook steaks in oil for 2 to 3 minutes per side or until golden brown and cooked to doneness. Remove and keep warm. Add soup and milk to skillet. Bring to a boil, stirring to loosen browned bits from pan. Serve gravy with steaks.

JUDITH MILLER, Fredericktown, OH

LIVER AND BACON

1 pound liver
¼ cup flour
1 teaspoon salt
Pepper to taste

Bacon fat
1 onion, sliced in rings
4 slices bacon, fried until crisp

Slice liver in ½-inch slices by about 3 inches long. Set in bowl of water for a few minutes, then drain and dry on towel. In bag or bowl, mix flour, salt, and pepper. Add liver and shake or toss to coat. In skillet, fry liver in bacon fat for about 8 minutes until crisp. Remove to platter. Add more fat and fry onion until tender soft. Serve liver topped with onion and 1 slice bacon.

ANN SHIRK, Shiloh, OH

Bacon-Liver Patties

1 pound beef liver
2 slices bacon (optional)
1 small onion
1 green pepper (optional)

1 teaspoon salt
⅛ teaspoon pepper
2 tablespoons flour
1 egg

Use grinder to grind liver, bacon, onion, and green pepper together. Mix in salt, pepper, flour, and egg. Drop by spoonful onto hot greased griddle. Serves 6.

"Since the liver is ground up, this makes it not so tough to eat."

Ruth Byler, Quaker City, OH

Baked Liver Patties

1 pound ground liver
1 slice bacon, chopped
½ cup breadcrumbs
¼ cup cream

½ teaspoon salt
⅛ teaspoon pepper
Bacon slices

Mix liver, chopped bacon, breadcrumbs, cream, salt, and pepper together. Shape into patties; wrap 1 slice bacon around each patty. Place in greased pan and bake at 425 degrees until brown, turning once.

"A delicious way to get your family to eat more liver!"

Mrs. Perry (Rebecca) Herschberger, Bear Lake, MI

Liver Patties

1 pound liver
1 egg
½ cup oats
1 teaspoon salt

Dash pepper
1 teaspoon mustard
1 tablespoon diced
onion (optional)

In blender, blend liver, egg, oats, salt, pepper, and mustard. Add onion before or after blending. Pour into hot greased skillet in patties like you would for pancakes. Cook each side for a couple of minutes. Make sandwichs with liver patties, lettuce, ketchup, etc. When you butcher, you can make 1-pound bags of cut-up liver pieces that are easy to thaw and use.

"This is a much nicer way to eat your liver! Eat some once a week or so to get your iron levels up during pregnancy."

Rosanne Hoover, Plymouth, OH

Tuna Patties

1 can tuna, drained
1 to 2 eggs
1 teaspoon minced onion
1 teaspoon mustard

1 teaspoon seasoned salt
½ teaspoon pepper
Enough cracker or bread
  crumbs to form patties

Mix all ingredients together and shape into patties. Fry in oil for a couple of minutes on each side until brown.

Malinda Gingerich, Spartansburg, PA

Pickled Pig Stomach

1 cleaned, peeled, cooked
   pig stomach*
1 part water

1 part vinegar
1 part sugar
1 medium onion, sliced

Prepare stomach and cut in bite-size pieces. In bowl, mix equal parts water, vinegar, and sugar. Stir well. Add chopped stomach and onion. Let soak for at least 4 hours. It is a good snack. This can also be made with heart and tongue.

*To clean a pig stomach, cut open from the tube opening lengthwise and empty any contents. Rinse well with hot water. Use plenty of salt for grip to tear the lining from the outside part. Keep the outside and toss the lining. Wash the outer stomach and boil in salt water until soft.

Mrs. Matthew C. Girod, Berne, IN

Pickled Heart

1 beef or deer heart
½ teaspoon salt
1½ cups water

⅛ cup apple cider vinegar
¾ teaspoon salt

In saucepan, cover heart with water and add ½ teaspoon salt. Boil until heart is cooked through and done. Chill. In bowl, stir together 1½ cups water, vinegar, and ¾ teaspoon salt. Slice cold heart into sealable container. Pour pickling mixture over top. Let sit for a day or two to pickle. You can adjust vinegar and salt to suit your taste.

Sarah Byler, Emienton, PA

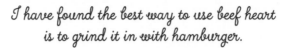

BEEF TONGUE

Place tongue in boiling water. Leave in hot water for approximately 30 minutes until you are able to scrape off the white coating. Put tongue and 1 cup water in pressure cooker under 10 pounds pressure for 45 minutes to tenderize tongue. Cut up in bite-size pieces. Dip in salt to eat.

ARLENE BONTREGER, Middlebury, IN

FRIED FROG LEGS

Only the hind legs of frogs can be eaten. Cut off feet and peel off skin, turning inside out. Wipe with cold damp cloth. Season with salt and pepper. Or, if desired, legs may be seasoned by soaking in mixture of lemon juice, salt, and pepper for 1 hour before proceeding. Roll in flour. Dip in well-beaten egg, diluted with a little water. Roll in cracker crumbs. They may be dipped in fritter batter instead, in which case you'd omit the flour and eggs. Fry in deep hot fat until golden brown, about 3 minutes. Serve with tartar sauce.

JUDITH MILLER, Fredericktown, OH

CHILLY DAY STEW

1 large carrot, chopped
3 onions
4 cups peeled and diced potatoes
2 tablespoons rice

2 tablespoons macaroni
1 teaspoon salt
2 cups heavy cream

In kettle ¼ full of water, place chopped carrot. While it starts to cook, chop onions. Add to kettle. Prepare your potatoes and add to kettle with rice, macaroni, and salt. Add more water if needed to cover all. Cook slowly until all is tender. When ready to serve, mix in cream (or substitute a combination of milk and butter). Let heat but do not boil. Serve with crackers or hot toast.

MARY KAUFFMAN, Albion, PA

Wintertime Supper

Ham or beef bone with some meat remaining
Peeled and diced potatoes or noodles

In saucepan, cover ham bone with water. Add potatoes. Add other vegetables if desired. Cook until potatoes are tender. Add salt and other seasoning if needed.

Mrs. Dan L. E. Miller, Dayton, PA

TIP:

What to Do with Leftovers?

Almost any kind of leftovers are good made into a soup by browning some butter in a kettle and adding the leftovers, stirring to warm and brown. Add enough milk to make enough servings for your family. Season with salt, pepper, and garlic powder. If you have Velveeta cheese, that would be a great addition. Be fearless! If you can't eat it, the dog probably can. But usually it turns out to be one of our favorite soups.

Mrs. Joseph Hochstetler, Danville, OH

Bean Soup

½ gallon milk
½ cup butter
½ cup navy beans with liquid

Salt and pepper to taste
1 loaf stale homemade bread

In saucepan, put a small amount of water in to cover bottom. Add milk and heat to boiling point. In small saucepan, brown butter to very dark color. Warm beans in another saucepan. When milk is to boiling point, add butter and remove from heat. Add salt and pepper. Add bread to desired "soupiness." Note: As the bread soaks, it will remove liquid from the soup. Add beans with their liquid. Sprinkle pepper on top to serve.

"This is the Amish church soup."

Miriam Byler, Spartansburg, PA

TIP:

When you need to stretch a pot of soup or casserole to feed a crowd, add a jar of beef or chicken broth.

Mrs. Henry J. Swartzentruber, Liberty, KY

Homemade Mushroom Soup

1 can mushrooms
¼ cup butter
¼ cup whole wheat flour

½ teaspoon salt
2 cups beef or chicken broth

Blend mushrooms in blender; set aside. In saucepan, melt butter. Add whole wheat flour and cook for 3 minutes. Add salt, broth, and mushrooms.

Toby Hertzler, Charlotte Court House, VA

Broccoli Cheese Soup

¾ cup chopped onion
3 tablespoons butter
6 cups water
3 tablespoons chicken base
1 teaspoon salt
8 ounces noodles

20 ounces frozen chopped broccoli or 1½ cups fresh chopped broccoli
¼ teaspoon garlic powder
Dash pepper
6 cups milk
½ to 1 pound Velveeta cheese

In large pot, sauté onion in butter. Add water, chicken base, salt, and noodles, then bring to a boil. Add broccoli, garlic powder, and pepper. Cook for 4 to 5 minutes. Add milk and cheese, stirring until cheese melts.

EDNA HERSHBERGER, Orrville, OH

Free Soup

After cooking vegetables, pour any water and leftover vegetable pieces into freezer container and freeze. When container is full, add tomato juice and seasonings to create a money-saving "free" soup.

AMANDA SWARTZENTRUBER, Dalton, OH

TIP:

To thicken and stretch soups, add instant potato flakes to the right consistency.
SALOMIE E. GLICK, Howard, PA

QUICK CREAMY POTATO SOUP

1 onion, diced
Butter

Leftover mashed potatoes
Milk

In saucepan, add onion and enough butter to coat well. Stir over heat until onion is partly softened. Add mashed potatoes and enough milk to bring it to preferred thickness.

ARLENE BONTREGER, Middlebury, IN

CREAM OF POTATO SOUP

½ cup butter
¾ cup flour
7 cups milk
4 teaspoons chicken base
2 teaspoons seasoned salt

¼ teaspoon pepper
4 cups shredded potatoes
1½ cups shredded carrots
1 cup shredded Velveeta
   or cheddar cheese

In 4-quart kettle, melt butter. Add flour and cook until bubbly. Gradually add milk, stirring constantly with whisk. Add chicken base, seasoned salt, and pepper. Heat until bubbly, stirring often. Meanwhile, in another kettle, cook potatoes and carrots in water until tender. Drain and add to hot milk mixture along with cheese. Stir until cheese is melted. Serve this with garden vegetable crackers.

"This is a delicious, budget-friendly soup that is simple to make."

ANNA HOSTETLER, Orwell, OH

Ham and Potato Soup

3 potatoes, diced or shredded
½ cup diced celery
3 tablespoons butter
1 small onion, chopped
2 tablespoons flour

4 cups milk
1½ teaspoons salt
⅛ teaspoon pepper
1 cup cubed ham
Velveeta cheese

Cook potatoes and celery in salted water; drain. In saucepan, melt butter and fry onion. Add flour and brown, then add milk. Cook for 1 minute. Add salt, pepper, ham, and enough cheese to suit your taste.

Emma Schwartz, Stanwood, MI

Cheesy Chicken Chowder

3 cups chicken broth
2 cups peeled and diced potatoes
1 cup diced carrots
1 cup diced celery
½ cup diced onion
1½ teaspoons salt
¼ teaspoon pepper
¼ cup butter
⅓ cup flour
2 cups milk
2 cups shredded cheddar cheese
2 cups diced cooked chicken

In 4-quart saucepan, bring broth to a boil. Reduce heat and add vegetables, salt, and pepper. Cover and simmer for 15 minutes until vegetables are tender. Meanwhile, in medium saucepan, melt butter. Add flour and mix well. Gradually stir in milk. Cook over low heat until slightly thickened. Stir in cheese and cook until melted. Add broth along with chicken. Cook and stir over low heat until heated through.

Mrs. Albert Summy, Meyersdale, PA

Instant Cream of Tomato Soup

1 (8 ounce) can no-
   salt tomato sauce
½ cup milk (we like rice milk)
¼ teaspoon oregano
¼ teaspoon basil
1 teaspoon onion powder

Mix all ingredients in saucepan and simmer for 3 minutes. Do not boil. You can add salt and adjust seasonings to suite your taste.

Rachel Hertzler, Charlotte Court House, VA

Hamburger Soup

2 tablespoons butter
1 pound ground beef
1 cup chopped onion
2 cups tomato juice
1 cup sliced carrots
1½ cups diced potatoes

½ cup chopped celery
1½ teaspoons salt
1 teaspoon seasoned salt
Dash pepper
4 cups milk
⅓ cup flour

In saucepan, melt butter. Add beef and onion and cook until browned. Stir in tomato juice, carrots, potatoes, celery, salt, seasoned salt, and pepper. In bowl, whisk together 1 cup milk and flour. Add to meat mixture and mix well. Add remaining milk and cook until heated, stirring frequently. Do not boil.

"This recipe is also good for using up leftover meat and vegetables."

Rachel Beiler, Leola, PA

Rivel Soup

4 cups milk
2 tablespoons flour

Heat milk to boiling. Meanwhile make a paste of the flour, then add to boiling milk and bring it to a boil again.

Rivels:
Flour
2 egg yolks

Add flour to egg yolks and mix until rivels form, much like crumbs. Add by sprinkling into boiling milk and cook until they are tender little dumplings.

"In the Great Depression, some people had only flour or corn flour and water to make soup."

Saloma D. Yoder, Mercer, MO

Pumpkin Soup

2 tablespoons butter
2 tablespoons chopped onion
1 large sprig parsley
⅛ teaspoon thyme
1 bay leaf
1 cup canned tomatoes

1 (16 ounce) can or 2 cups pumpkin
2 cups chicken broth
1 tablespoon flour
1 cup milk
1 teaspoon salt
⅛ teaspoon pepper

In large saucepan, melt butter. Add onion, parsley, thyme, and bay leaf. Simmer for 5 minutes. Add tomatoes, pumpkin, and broth. Cover and simmer for 30 minutes, stirring occasionally. Remove bay leaf and puree soup mixture in blender. In bowl, blend flour and milk. Stir into soup. Add salt and pepper. Bring soup to a boil. Other seasonings can be added to suit your taste. Serve with crackers.

Note: before adding flour and milk, the soup can be canned in pint or quart canning jars at 10 pounds pressure for 35 minutes.

MARY JOYCE PETERSHEIM, Fredericktown, OH

DESSERTS

*For he hath said, I will never
leave thee, nor forsake thee.*

HEBREWS 13:5

Easy Gelatin Dessert

1 (3 ounce) package gelatin mix (any flavor)
2 cups boiling water
2 cups plain yogurt

Dissolve gelatin in boiling water. Refrigerate until it just starts to set. Mix in yogurt. Refrigerate until set.

Nora Miller, Millersburg, OH

Egg Custard

2 quarts milk
12 egg yolks, beaten
3 whole eggs, beaten
½ cup sugar

⅓ cup maple syrup
Pinch salt
1 teaspoon vanilla
Cinnamon (optional)

In pot, heat milk to scald. Remove from heat and add yolks and eggs. Add sugar, maple syrup, salt, and vanilla. Divide into 12 jars or ramekins. Add a sprinkle of cinnamon to each. Set jars in cake pan. Heat some water to boiling and pour into pan to halfway up jars. Bake at 350 degrees for 1 hour. Cool completely before serving.

Mrs. Reuben (Anna) Lapp, Rockville, IN

Coffee Pudding

6 cups milk
1 cup sugar
Pinch salt
1 rounded tablespoon
    instant coffee

¾ cup Therm Flo
1 tablespoon butter
1 tablespoon vanilla

In saucepan, heat 5 cups milk, sugar, salt, and coffee to boiling point. Mix remaining 1 cup milk and Therm Flo, then add to heated milk, stirring well. Remove from heat and add butter and vanilla.

Mrs. Reuben (Anna) Lapp, Rockville, IN

CARAMEL APPLE PUDDING

¾ cup flour
1 teaspoon baking powder
1 teaspoon cinnamon
½ cup sugar
¼ teaspoon salt
½ cup milk
1½ cups chopped apples
½ cup chopped nuts

In bowl, mix flour, baking powder, cinnamon, sugar, and salt. Slowly add milk, stirring until smooth. Add apples and nuts and mix to coat. Spread batter in 9x9-inch dish.

SAUCE:
¾ cup water
¾ cup brown sugar
¼ cup margarine

In saucepan, bring water to a boil. Add brown sugar and margarine, stirring until well blended. Pour over batter. Bake at 375 degrees for 40 to 50 minutes. Serve warm, topped with ice cream or whipped cream. Also delicious cold.

ALVIN JR. AND RUTH FISHER, Berlin, PA

MAPLE SPONGE PUDDING

2 cups brown sugar
2 cups hot water
½ teaspoon maple flavoring
1 large package
   unflavored gelatin
½ cup water
1 package vanilla instant
   pudding mix or
   homemade equivalent
1 cup heavy whipping cream
Sliced bananas
Chopped nuts

In saucepan, bring brown sugar, hot water, and maple flavoring to a boil for 10 minutes. In bowl, dissolve gelatin in ½ cup water. Let sit for a couple of minutes, then add to hot mixture. Let cool until firm. Mix pudding according to package directions. In bowl, whip heavy cream to peak and fold into pudding. In individual serving dishes, layer sponge and pudding with sprinkles of bananas and nuts.

FANNIE MILLER, Pierpont, OH

Vanilla Pudding

3½ cups milk
¾ cup sugar
⅓ cup cornstarch
½ teaspoon salt

2 eggs, beaten
½ cup cold milk
1 tablespoon butter
1 teaspoon vanilla

In saucepan, scald milk. In bowl, mix sugar, cornstarch, and salt. Add eggs and cold milk. Stir into hot milk until it thickens. Remove from heat and add butter and vanilla. This is delicious layered with whipped topping, bananas, and crushed graham crackers.

Mrs. Chester Miller, Centerville, PA

Country Cobbler

4 cups fresh fruit
½ cup sugar
1 stick butter
1½ cups flour

2 cups sugar
4 teaspoons baking powder
½ teaspoon salt
1½ cups milk

Mix fruit and ½ cup sugar. Set aside. In 350-degree oven, melt butter in 9x13-inch baking pan. In bowl, sift flour, 2 cups sugar, baking powder, and salt. Add milk and mix well. Pour batter into pan on top of butter; do not mix. Drop spoonfuls of fruit on batter. Bake at 350 degrees for 50 minutes.

Esther Schwartz, Portland, IN

Iowa Goody

1 cup flour
1 cup sugar
1 teaspoon baking soda

1 egg
1 cup fruit with juice

Stir all ingredients together just enough to mix. Pour into small baking dish and bake at 375 degrees for 20 to 30 minutes. Serve hot with milk. Note: if your fruit is very sweet, you can use only ½ cup sugar.

FANNIE MILLER, Pierpont, OH

Frozen Strawberry Fluff

2 cups graham cracker crumbs
5 tablespoons butter, melted
2 egg whites
1 tablespoon vanilla

2 cups chopped fresh or
  frozen strawberries
1½ cups sugar
1 cup heavy cream, whipped

Mix graham cracker crumbs and butter. Press into 9x13-inch pan. Bake at 350 degrees for 8 minutes. Cool. In bowl, beat egg whites and vanilla until frothy. Gradually beat in strawberries and sugar. Beat at high speed for 12 to 15 minutes until mixture is fluffy with high volume. Fold in whipped cream. Freeze overnight.

DANIEL STOLTZFUS, Nottingham, PA

CARAMEL CREAM TAPIOCA

4 cups water
Dash salt
¾ cup tapioca
¾ to 1 cup sugar
1 teaspoon vanilla

½ teaspoon maple flavoring
½ cup chopped nuts
2 tablespoons butter
Whipped cream

In saucepan, bring water and salt to a boil. Add tapioca, stirring constantly. Cook until clear. Add sugar, vanilla, and maple flavoring. In small frying pan, brown nuts in butter. Cool. Add nuts on top of whipped cream to each serving of tapioca. You can also crush any kind of candy bar on top of each serving.

JUDITH MILLER, Fredericktown, OH

FROZEN LIME PIE

1 tablespoon unflavored gelatin
¾ cup sugar
⅛ teaspoon salt
1 cup milk
⅓ cup fresh lime juice
1½ teaspoons lime zest

Few drops green food coloring
1 cup heavy cream, whipped
1 egg white
1 (9 inch) graham cracker
  crumb crust

In saucepan, mix gelatin, sugar, and salt. Add milk and heat until gelatin and sugar are dissolved. Chill until mixture begins to thicken. Add lime juice, zest, and food coloring. Fold in whipped cream. In bowl, beat egg white until it holds stiff peaks. Fold into gelatin mixture. Spoon into crumb crust. Freeze. Serve with additional whipped cream if desired. Note: reconstituted lime juice may be used if fresh isn't available.

MARY JOYCE PETERSHEIM, Fredericktown, OH

Apple Pie on a Cookie Sheet

2 cups pastry flour
1 teaspoon salt
5 tablespoons sugar
⅔ cup plus 1 tablespoon
    shortening or ⅔ cup lard

4 to 5 tablespoons cold water
1 quart apple pie filling
Sugar

In bowl, mix pastry flour, salt, and sugar. Cut in shortening until crumbly. Add cold water and mix until dough comes together. Roll out dough and cut to fit 9x13-inch pan. Spread apple pie filling on top of crust. Cut remaining dough into strips or cookie cutter shapes and lay over pie filling. Sprinkle with sugar. Bake at 375 degrees for 35 to 45 minutes or until golden brown.

MRS. CHESTER MILLER, Centerville, PA

Chocolate Sponge Pie

2 egg yolks	¼ scant cup flour
1⅓ cups milk	1 teaspoon vanilla
¾ cup sugar	2 egg whites
¼ cup cocoa powder	1 (9 inch) unbaked pie shell

Beat egg yolks, then beat in milk. Sift together sugar, cocoa, and flour. Add to egg mixture. Add vanilla. Beat egg whites to stiff but not dry. Fold into first mixture. Pour into pie shell. Bake at 375 degrees for 25 to 30 minutes until set.

Lillian J. Yoder, Grantsville, MD

Ground Cherry Pie

2½ cups ground cherries
   (discard husks)
1 (9 inch) unbaked pie shell
½ cup brown sugar

4 tablespoons flour
2 tablespoons water
3 tablespoons sugar
2 tablespoons butter

Wash ground cherries and place in pie shell. In bowl, mix brown sugar and 1 tablespoon flour; sprinkle over cherries. Sprinkle water on top. In bowl, mix remaining 3 tablespoons flour and sugar. Cut in butter until crumbly. Top cherries with crumbs. Bake at 425 degrees for 15 minutes. Reduce heat to 375 degrees and continue to bake for 25 minutes.

Mrs. Robert Yoder, Stanwood, MI

Oatmeal Pie

3 eggs
¼ cup butter, melted
½ cup sugar
¼ cup warm water
1 cup maple syrup

¾ cup oats
1½ teaspoons vanilla
½ teaspoon salt
1 (9 inch) unbaked pie shell

Mix eggs, butter, sugar, warm water, and maple syrup. Stir in oats, vanilla, and salt. Pour into pie shell. Bake at 350 degrees for 1 hour.

"Delicious! Tastes similar to pecan pie."

EllaMae Hilty, Berne, IN

Never-Fail Piecrust

3 cups flour
1½ teaspoons salt
1 cup lard

½ cup milk
2 teaspoons vinegar

In mixing bowl, combine flour and salt. Mix in lard until crumbly. In small bowl, mix milk and vinegar. Add to flour mixture and mix well until it comes together. Chill before rolling out.

Amanda Coblentz, Portland, IN

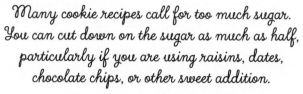

CLASSIC CHOCOLATE CHIP COOKIES

9 cups flour
4 teaspoons baking powder
4 teaspoons baking soda
3 cups margarine, softened
3 cups brown sugar
4 packages vanilla instant
    pudding mix
1 cup sugar
4 teaspoons vanilla
8 eggs
4 (12 ounce) packages
    chocolate chips
1 cup chopped walnuts
    (optional)

In large bowl, combine flour, baking powder, and baking soda. Set aside. In another bowl, beat margarine, brown sugar, pudding mix, sugar, and vanilla together until smooth. Beat in eggs. Gradually add flour mixture. Stir in chocolate chips and walnuts. Drop by teaspoonful onto baking sheet. Bake at 350 degrees for 10 to 12 minutes. Yield: 9 dozen cookies. Note: you can use butterscotch pudding and butterscotch baking chips for a different flavor.

"These are our favorite cookies."

MALINDA HOSTETLER, West Salem, OH

Old-Fashioned Three-Ingredient Peanut Butter Cookies

1 cup sugar
1 cup peanut butter
1 egg

In bowl, mix sugar, peanut butter, and egg together until smooth. Roll into 1-inch balls. Place on parchment-lined baking sheet and press down with back of fork in two crosswise directions to form crisscross pattern. Bake at 350 degrees for 12 minutes.

Sarah M. Swartzentruber, Polk, OH

Triple Treat Cookies

1 cup shortening
1 cup sugar
1 cup brown sugar
2 eggs
1 cup peanut butter
2 teaspoons baking soda
1 teaspoon vanilla
½ teaspoon salt
1 cup flour
2 cups oats
1 cup chocolate chips

Blend shortening, sugar, and brown sugar. Add eggs, then peanut butter. Mix in baking soda, vanilla, salt, flour, and oats. Mix in chocolate chips. Roll dough into balls and put on greased cookie sheet. Bake at 350 degrees for 10 to 12 minutes.

Susan Schwartz, Berne, IN

Cake Mix Cookies

Add 2 eggs and ½ cup oil to any flavor cake mix and you have a quick dough for a batch of cookies. Add raisins, nuts, coconut, or chocolate chips if desired. Drop by teaspoonful onto slightly greased cookie sheets. Bake at 350 degrees for 8 to 10 minutes.

Katie Zook, Apple Creek, OH

CAN'T-LEAVE-ALONE BARS

1 box yellow cake mix
2 eggs
⅓ cup vegetable oil

1 can sweetened condensed milk
½ cup butter
1 cup chocolate chips

In bowl, mix cake mix, eggs, and oil. Pour half of batter in greased 9x13-inch pan. In saucepan, cook condensed milk, butter, and chocolate chips until melted. Pour over batter and top with remaining batter. Bake at 350 degrees for 20 to 30 minutes.

JOSIE D. MILLER, Dayton, PA

GREEN TOMATO BARS

4 cups finely chopped
  green tomatoes
2 cups brown sugar
¾ cup butter, softened
1½ cups flour

1 teaspoon baking soda
1 teaspoon salt
2 cups oats
½ cup nuts, chopped
1 cup blueberries (optional)

In saucepan, cook tomatoes and 1 cup brown sugar over low heat until tomatoes are softened and juicy. In mixing bowl, cream butter and remaining brown sugar; add flour, baking soda, salt, oats, and nuts. Grease 9x13-inch pan. Measure out 2½ cups dough and press into bottom of pan. Spread tomato mixture, including juice, on top. Sprinkle blueberries over tomatoes. Crumble remaining dough and sprinkle over all. Bake at 375 degrees for 30 to 35 minutes. Yield: 16 servings.

"Great way to use up green tomatoes at the end of the growing season. The blueberries help to hide the green from the kids and make the bars more eye appealing. Still just as yummy without the berries, though."

GRANOLIES

1½ cups granola
¾ cup flour
1 teaspoon baking powder
¼ teaspoon baking soda
¼ teaspoon salt
½ cup chopped nuts or dates

½ cup butter
½ cup brown sugar
¼ cup molasses
1 egg
½ teaspoon vanilla

In bowl, combine granola, flour, baking powder, baking soda, salt, and nuts. In another bowl, cream together butter, brown sugar, molasses, egg, and vanilla. Add dry mixture and mix well. Spread in ungreased 9x9-inch pan. Bake at 350 degrees for 25 minutes or until done.

MALINDA GINGERICH, Spartansburg, PA

GOOD RICH BARS

1 cup butter
4 large eggs
3 cups brown sugar
1½ teaspoons baking powder

½ teaspoon salt
1 tablespoon vanilla
2⅔ cups flour
1 cup chocolate chips

In mixing bowl, beat butter, eggs, and brown sugar until fluffy. Add baking powder, salt, vanilla, and flour. Pour in greased cookie sheet. Sprinkle with chocolate chips. Bake at 350 degrees for 20 to 25 minutes.

S. BYLER, Reynoldsville, PA

ZUCCHINI BARS

1 cup vegetable oil
2 cups sugar
4 eggs
2 teaspoons vanilla
2 cups shredded zucchini
2 cups flour

1 teaspoon baking powder
1 teaspoon baking soda
1 teaspoon cinnamon
¼ teaspoon salt
1 cup chopped walnuts

In mixing bowl, blend oil, sugar, eggs, and vanilla. Add zucchini, flour, baking powder, baking soda, cinnamon, salt, and walnuts. Mix well. Put in greased cookie sheet with sides. Bake at 350 degrees for 30 minutes.

FROSTING:

8 ounces cream cheese, softened
¼ cup butter or
     margarine, softened

2 teaspoons milk
½ teaspoon vanilla
2 cups powdered sugar

Beat all ingredients together until smooth. Spread over cooled bars.

"I shred zucchini and freeze it for recipes like this one."

RACHEL BEILER, Leola, PA

Easy Apple Cake

½ cup shortening
1 stick margarine
1 cup sugar
2 eggs

2 cups sifted flour
1 can apple pie filling
Powdered sugar

In bowl, cream together shortening and margarine. Add sugar gradually, mixing well. Add eggs and beat well. Gradually add flour. Measure ½ cup batter and set aside. Spread remaining batter in greased 9x13-inch pan. Top with apple pie filling. Drop pinches of ½ cup batter on top of apples. Bake at 350 degrees for 40 minutes. While cake is still warm, dust with powdered sugar.

Sarah M. Swartzentruber, Polk, OH

Depression Cake

1 cup water
½ teaspoon salt
1 cup sugar
½ cup lard or shortening
1 cup raisins
1 teaspoon cinnamon
1 teaspoon allspice

1 teaspoon nutmeg
¼ teaspoon ground cloves
1 teaspoon baking
  soda, dissolved in 1
  tablespoon water
1¾ cups flour
Nuts or candied fruit (optional)

In saucepan, bring water to a boil. Add salt, sugar, lard, raisins, cinnamon, allspice, nutmeg, and cloves. Bring all to a boil, then let stand to cool. Stir in baking soda paste and flour. Add nuts. Place in greased 9x13-inch pan. Bake for 30 minutes at 350 degrees. Serve with whipped cream or ice cream with caramel icing.

Shortcake

2 cups flour
1 cup sugar
2 teaspoons baking powder
¼ cup shortening
1 egg, beaten

Milk
1 quart canned unsweetened
  cherries or strawberries
2 tablespoons sugar
2 tablespoons flour

In bowl, blend 2 cups flour, 1 cup sugar, baking powder, and shortening. Mix in egg. Add enough milk to make a thick batter. Place cherries in 9x13-inch pan. Sprinkle with 2 tablespoons sugar and 2 tablespoons flour. Then spoon batter over top. Bake at 350 degrees for 30 to 35 minutes.

ERNEST AND MARY EICHER, Montgomery, MI

Angel Food Cake

1 cup cake flour	½ teaspoon salt
1½ cups sugar	1½ teaspoons cream of tartar
1½ cups egg whites	1 teaspoon almond flavoring

Sift together cake lour and ¾ cup sugar 3 times. Set aside. Beat egg whites until frothy, then add salt and cream of tartar. Beat until it stands in peaks. Add remaining ¾ cup sugar about 3 tablespoons at a time, beating well with each addition. Lightly fold in flour mixture, adding about ½ cup at a time. Add almond flavoring. Bake in ungreased tube pan or 2 loaf pans at 375 degrees for 35 to 40 minutes until done. It is done when top is dark golden brown and looks dry.

Tips for making angel food cake:

- Have all ingredients at room temperature.
- Use cake flour only.
- Egg whites should contain no trace of egg yolk.
- Make sure the sugar is clean when beaten with egg whites. Any trace of flour could damage the meringue.
- Fold in flour and sugar mixture gently with spatula. Do NOT beat.
- Bake in ungreased tube pan and turn upside down to cool.
- Be careful not to overbake.

MIRIAM BYLER, Spartansburg, PA

Glorified Gingerbread

2 cups sifted flour
1 cup sugar
½ teaspoon ginger
½ teaspoon cinnamon
½ cup shortening

1 egg, beaten
½ cup molasses
½ teaspoon salt
1 teaspoon baking soda
½ cup sour milk or buttermilk

In bowl, sift flour, then measure 2 cups. Add sugar, ginger, and cinnamon and sift again. Rub shortening into mixture to make fine crumbs. Take out ½ cup crumbs and set aside for topping. To flour mixture, add egg, molasses, salt, baking soda, and milk, beating until well blended and batter is smooth. Pour into greased 8x8-inch pan. Sprinkle top with reserved crumbs. Bake at 350 degrees for 45 minutes.

JUDITH MILLER, Fredericktown, OH

TIP:

To keep your cake from getting holes, run a knife through the cake batter after you have finished mixing it. It will take out any air bubbles that could cause the cake to collapse.

MARTHA MILLER, Decatur, IN

Black Magic Cake

2¼ cups flour
2 cups sugar
½ cup cocoa powder
2 teaspoons baking powder
1 teaspoon baking soda

1 teaspoon salt
½ cup oil
2 eggs
1 cup sour milk
1 cup strong hot coffee

In large mixing bowl, combine flour, sugar, cocoa, baking powder, baking soda, and salt. Make a well in center and add oil, eggs, and milk. Beat well. Add hot coffee and mix well. Pour into greased and floured 9x13-inch pan. Bake at 350 degrees for 30 to 40 minutes or until toothpick inserted into center comes out clean.

AMANDA SWARTZENTRUBER, Dalton, OH

HOMEMADE CHOCOLATE CAKE MIX

20 cups flour
18 cups sugar
10 teaspoons salt

10 teaspoons baking powder
20 teaspoons baking soda
7½ cups cocoa powder

In large bowl, whisk all together until well mixed. Store in airtight container(s).

To bake a 9x13-inch cake:

4½ cups cake mix
1 cup oil
1 cup milk

2 eggs
1 cup coffee or water

Mix all and beat until well incorporated. Pour into greased and floured 9x13-inch pan. Bake at 350 degrees for 35 to 40 minutes until cake tests done.

ESTHER L. MILLER, Fredericktown, OH

QUICK CARAMEL FROSTING

4 tablespoons milk
4 tablespoons brown sugar

2 tablespoons butter
Powdered sugar

Combine milk, brown sugar, and butter in saucepan and boil for 1 minute. Thicken as desired with powdered sugar.

ESTHER SCHWARTZ, Portland, IN

Grandma Emma's Favorite Frosting

1 cup milk
1 to 2 cups sugar

2 tablespoons margarine

In 3- to 4-quart kettle, cook milk, sugar, and margarine until sugar dissolves. Turn heat down and add more margarine if it wants to boil up over top of kettle. Boil for about 12 minutes; DON'T STIR. Then test by dipping spoon into mixture and dropping into glass of cold water. When it stays together in a misshapen ball, it is ready. Don't wait until it stays together in a hard ball. Remove from heat and cool. Don't stir anytime while boiling or cooling. When frosting has cooled to lukewarm, start stirring it. Keep stirring until it gets white and runny, then put on cake immediately. It will harden. If it doesn't get hard enough, it didn't boil long enough. If it hardens as soon as it starts to run, you boiled it too long. You can crumble it onto the cake and try again another time.

MIRIAM BYLER, Spartansburg, PA

Peanut Butter Frosting

3 ounces cream cheese, softened
¼ cup creamy peanut butter
2 cups powdered sugar

2 tablespoons milk
½ teaspoon vanilla

In mixing bowl, beat together cream cheese and peanut butter. Add powdered sugar, milk, and vanilla, beating until well mixed. Very good spread on chocolate cake. Store in refrigerator.

MRS. REUBEN N. BYLER, Dayton, PA

TIP:

When baking, if I have leftover frosting, I put it between 2 graham crackers. The children love this treat.

MRS. CHESTER MILLER, Centerville, PA

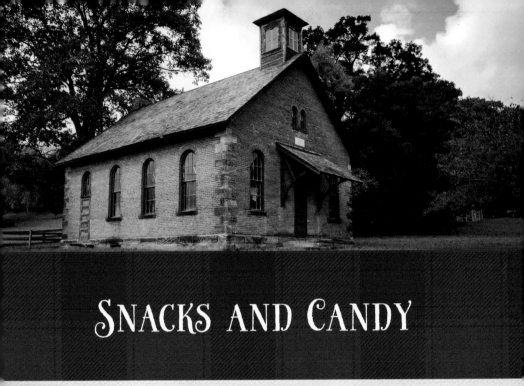

Snacks and Candy

*When we have nothing left but God,
we will find that He is enough.*

AMISH PROVERB

Apple Dip

8 ounces cream cheese
¼ cup brown sugar
⅛ cup powdered sugar

2 tablespoons milk
2 teaspoons vanilla

Whip cream cheese until smooth. Add brown sugar, powdered sugar, milk, and vanilla and beat until smooth. Enjoy with fresh apple slices.

Ruth Yoder, Berlin, PA

Homemade Energy Bars

2 cups peanut butter
1½ cups honey
3 cups oats
3 cups crisp rice cereal
1½ cups coconut

1 cup ground flaxseeds
1½ cups chocolate chips
1½ cups chopped pecans
3 teaspoons vanilla

Mix all together and press in jelly roll pan. No baking required. Quick and easy to enjoy.

Lizzie Hostetler, Homerville, OH

Coconut Oil Granola Bars

⅔ cup coconut oil, melted
⅔ cup peanut butter
½ cup honey
2 cups oats

2 cups extras of choice
(chocolate chips, chia seeds, coconut, chopped nuts, sunflower seeds, etc.)

In mixing bowl, mix coconut oil, peanut butter, and honey. Add oats and extras, mixing well. Press into 9x9-inch pan and refrigerate until hardened. Store in refrigerator.

Benjamin Yoder Jr., Narvon, PA

Roasted Butternut Seeds

2 cups butternut squash seeds
2 to 3 tablespoons olive oil
1 teaspoon sea salt flakes

Crushed dried chilies or
chili powder to taste

Pull all fibers away from seeds; discard. Put seeds in bowl and sprinkle with olive oil and toss to coat. Sprinkle with salt and chilies and toss to mix. Spread seeds in roasting pan and cook at 400 degrees for 15 to 20 minutes. Stir after 10 minutes so both sides get toasted. Keep checking toward end of cook time so they don't burn. When crisp and toasted, remove from oven and serve as snacks, on salads, or on top of pasta or risotto.

Elizabeth Swarey, Charlotte Courthouse, VA

Roasted Pumpkin Seeds

Wash seeds and dry a little. Put on baking sheet in single layer. Sprinkle with salt. Roast in oven at 150 to 200 degrees for 12 to 15 minutes, stirring occasionally until done to your liking. We like them crispy.

Benjamin Yoder Jr., Narvon, PA

TIP:

Eat your pumpkin seeds instead of throwing them out. A great remedy to expel worms in people and animals.
Katie Hoover, East Earl, PA

CASHEW CRUNCH

1 cup butter
1 cup sugar

1¾ cups cashew pieces

In hot skillet, melt butter. Add sugar and cashews, stirring until caramel colored. Pour on ungreased cookie sheet and press out as flat as you can. Cool then break apart.

JOSIE D. MILLER, Dayton, PA

EASY ENERGY BITES

3 cups quick oats
1 cup peanut butter

½ cup honey
Chocolate chips

Mix all ingredients together. Press into pan and cut into squares or roll into balls. No need to bake.

FANNIE GINGERICH, Navarre, OH

SNACK CRACKERS

½ cup butter
2 cups grated cheddar cheese
1½ cups sifted flour

½ teaspoon salt
1 tablespoon chives

Cream together butter and cheese. Add flour, salt, and chives. Mix well. Roll into 1-inch balls. Place on baking sheet lined with parchment paper. Flatten each ball with bottom of glass. Prick top with fork. Bake at 350 degrees for 12 to 15 minutes. Yield: 5 dozen crackers.

"These taste similar to Cheez-Its and are an inexpensive treat, especially if you make your own cheese and butter."

S. BEILER, Woodward, PA

Spicy Seasoned Pretzels

1 bag pretzels
1 package ranch powder mix
2 teaspoons cayenne pepper
1 cup oil

Place pretzels in large bowl. In small bowl, mix ranch powder and cayenne into oil. Pour over pretzels. Stir well to coat. Bake at 200 degrees for 30 minutes, stirring well every 10 minutes.

Martha Miller, Decatur, IN

Sweet-and-Salty Pretzels

3 pounds pretzel sticks
1 cup butter
1½ cups brown sugar
½ teaspoon salt

Put pretzels in large bowl. In saucepan, combine butter, brown sugar, and salt. Stir constantly and cook until caramelized. Pour over pretzels and mix well to coat. Spread on baking sheets and bake at 350 degrees for 5 minutes, stir, then bake for 6 more minutes.

Elizabeth Miller, Millersburg, OH

Healthy Sweet Potato Chips

1½ pounds sweet potatoes
⅓ cup olive oil

1 teaspoon salt
1 teaspoon pepper

Peel potatoes and slice on mandolin into paper-thin rounds. Combine olive oil, salt, and pepper in large mixing bowl, add sliced potatoes, and toss to coat. Spread slices in single layer on 2 parchment-lined baking sheets; leave space around slices. Bake at 400 degrees for 10 to 12 minutes on each side, turning once until golden brown. Remove from oven and cool chips on cooling rack for 5 to 10 minutes. They will crisp up a little more as they cool.

Mrs. Henry J. Swartzentruber, Liberty, KY

CARAMEL POPCORN

2 cups brown sugar
2 sticks margarine
½ cup corn syrup
1 teaspoon salt

1 teaspoon baking soda
1 teaspoon vanilla
12 quarts unsalted popcorn

In saucepan, bring brown sugar, margarine, corn syrup, and salt to a boil. Mix in baking soda and vanilla. Pour over popcorn and stir to coat well. Spread into roaster and bake at 200 degrees for 1 hour, stirring every 15 minutes.

LYDIANNE K. HERTZLER, Charlotte Courthouse, VA

HONEY POPCORN NUT CRUNCH

½ cup butter
½ cup honey

3 quarts popcorn
1 cup chopped nuts

In saucepan, melt butter and mix in honey, heating gently until combined. In bowl, combine popcorn and nuts. Pour butter mixture over popcorn and mix well. Spread on cookie sheet in thin layer. Bake at 350 degrees for 10 to 15 minutes or until crisp. Cool thoroughly then bag in individual serving bags.

KATIE ZOOK, Apple Creek, OH

Healthy Fudge

1 cup carob powder or
  cocoa powder
1 cup oats
1 cup sunflower seeds

1 cup peanut butter
1 cup honey
1 cup coconut

In bowl, mix carob powder, oats, sunflower seeds, peanut butter, and honey. Roll into balls, then roll in coconut to coat.

Toby and Rachel Hertzler, Charlotte Court House, VA

Snickers Copycat

1 cup corn syrup
1 cup brown sugar
1 cup peanut butter
2 cups crisp rice cereal

2 cups peanuts
16 ounces chocolate
  candy coating

In saucepan, cook corn syrup and brown sugar for 5 minutes. Add peanut butter and mix until smooth. Remove from heat and add cereal and peanuts. Flatten out onto greased baking sheet. Cool. Cut into bars. Melt chocolate in microwave or over double boiler, stirring until smooth. Dip bars in chocolate to fully coat. Set on waxed paper to dry.

Josephine Eicher, Montgomery, MI

Maple Syrup Suckers

12 ounces maple syrup
4 ounces light corn syrup
Butter the size of a pea

Spray heat resistant sucker molds with cooking spray. In saucepan, combine maple syrup, corn syrup, and butter. Cook to hard-crack stage or 295 degrees. Pour into sucker molds and insert sticks, or pour onto waxed paper–lined pan and break into pieces when cold. As soon as they're cooled, wrap suckers in bags or they'll get sticky.

"These are good sellers at roadside stands."

Isaac Schwartz, Stanwood, MI

Fruit Juice Finger Gel

8 tablespoons unflavored gelatin
2 quarts fruit juice
½ teaspoon stevia or to taste

In saucepan, dissolve gelatin in 2 cups juice, then heat to boiling point. Remove from heat and add remaining juice and stevia. Pour into flat-bottom pans and refrigerate. When fully set, cut as desired. Note: sweetened juice may not need any stevia.

Esther Coblentz, Fredericksburg, OH

CANNING AND CURING

*The thief cometh not, but for to steal, and to kill,
and to destroy: I am come that they might have life,
and that they might have it more abundantly.*

JOHN 10:10

Canned Grape Juice

Fill jars ⅓ full of fresh picked and washed grapes. Fill jars with water. Affix lids and cold pack jars for 5 minutes. You can add stevia or Sucanat to your taste preference before canning or after opening a sealed jar and before serving. When opening a jar for juice, drain out the juice and add an equal amount of water. Then put the grapes in a food mill to mash. Use the puree to help thicken a pie or pudding.

Katie Petersheim, Lakeview, MI

Simple Fruit Canning

Fill jars with fruit and syrup. Leave no air space in jars. Screw lids on tight. Set jars in 5-gallon pail and cover completely with water. Set pails in icehouse. Should keep over winter without canning under heat to seal.

Arlene Bontreger, Middlebury, IN

TIP:

Adding a peach pit or two to each jar of peaches when canning adds flavor and more vibrant color. Put them in the jar first, then add peaches and can as usual.

Mrs. Bethany Martin, Homer City, PA

APPLESAUCE

After you have canned your apple pie filling, you have a bunch of peelings and cores left. Don't throw them out. Cook this in some water, then put it through a strainer. You will get a dark applesauce that works perfectly for making apple butter. You will be surprised how much sauce you get.

EMMA KURTZ, Smicksburg, PA

John Llyod and Susan Yoder, Newaygo, MI

APPLE JELLY

Use apple peelings from making apple pie, applesauce, or other apple dish. Red apples are best and make a nice pink jelly. Cook peelings in a little water. Strain and use juice to make jelly as directed on Sure-Jell package for apple jelly.

MRS. DAN L. E. MILLER, Dayton, PA

PEACH PEELING JELLY

Save your peach peelings and pits, filling a 6- or 8-quart kettle. Add water to cover and cook. Boil for about 10 minutes. Pour into strainer or colander and let drip. Will yield 2 to 3 quarts juice. Make jelly as directed on Sure-Jell package for apple or pear jelly. Very tasty.

ROSIE SCHWARTZ, Salem, IN

MRS. BETHANY MARTIN, Homer City, PA

DANDELION JELLY

1 quart dandelion blossoms
 without any stems attached
1 quart water
1 package pectin

1 teaspoon lemon or
 orange extract
4½ cups sugar

Pick dandelion blossoms first thing in the morning. Boil blossoms in water for 3 minutes. Drain off 3 cups liquid. Add pectin, lemon extract, and sugar to liquid. Boil for 3 minutes. Seal into jars. The taste resembles honey.

ROSIE SCHWARTZ, Salem, IN

Pickled Watermelon Rind

Watermelon rind
1½ cups sugar
½ cup vinegar

1 cup water
⅛ teaspoon salt
1 tablespoon whole cloves

Trim off all red watermelon from rind. Peel rind, then cube. Pack rind in jars. In saucepan, combine sugar, vinegar, water, salt, and cloves. Boil for 20 minutes. Strain out whole cloves and pour over rinds in jars. Affix 2-piece lids and seal in water bath for 20 minutes.

BENUEL L. AND BARBARA Z. KING, Myerstown, PA

Cinnamon Cucumber Pickles

A good recipe to use up cucumbers that have gotten overly large.

2 gallons (approximately
    7 pounds) extra-large
    cucumbers, peeled, cored,
    and sliced ½ inch thick
2 gallons water
2 cups pickling lime
1 cup vinegar

1 tablespoon alum
1 bottle red or green
    food coloring
6 cups vinegar
2 cups water
10 cups sugar
8 sticks cinnamon

In large bowl or crock, soak cucumbers in 2 gallons water with lime for 24 hours. Drain and rinse well; place in large saucepan. Combine 1 cup vinegar, alum, and food coloring. Pour over cucumbers and add enough water to cover cucumbers. Heat and simmer for 2 hours. Drain and place in bowl. Make a syrup with 6 cups vinegar, 2 cups water, sugar, and cinnamon; bring to a boil. Pour syrup over cucumbers and let stand overnight. Drain and reheat syrup; pour back over cucumbers and let stand overnight. Do this for 3 days. On third day, pack cucumbers with syrup in pint jars and seal in hot water bath for 5 minutes.

CRISP DILL PICKLES

2 cups sugar
2 cups water
2 cups vinegar
3 teaspoons salt

3 quarts cucumbers
3 heads dill
3 cloves garlic

In saucepan, heat sugar, water, vinegar, and salt. Wash and cut cucumbers in desired pieces. Place 1 head dill and 1 clove garlic in each 3-quart jar, then fill with cucumbers. Pour hot mixture over cucumbers to fill jars. Seal and cold pack jars just to boiling point, then remove jars to cool.

MRS. ALBERT SUMMY, Meyersdale, PA

DELAWARE MIXED PICKLES

1 gallon ground or diced
   green tomatoes
½ cup salt
1 quart cooked lima or
   navy beans, drained
1 quart chopped onion
1 quart corn
1 dozen small sweet
   pickles, sliced

6 red peppers, chopped
6 green peppers, chopped
1 ounce celery seed
2 ounces mustard seed
2 tablespoons ground mustard
1 teaspoon turmeric
3 pounds sugar
1 quart vinegar

In bowl or crock, mix tomatoes and salt. Let stand for 2 hours. Drain and put in stockpot with remaining ingredients. Bring to a boil for 5 minutes. Pack into hot, sterile jars and seal. Any vegetables can be substituted or added.

I like to make this in the fall when the green tomatoes won't ripen any more and there are other vegetables to clean out of the garden.

EMMA KURTZ, Smicksburg, PA

BREAD AND BUTTER PICKLES

1 gallon thinly sliced
  fresh cucumbers
4 small onions, thinly
  sliced or chopped
2 green peppers, chopped
¼ cup salt
1 quart water

5 cups sugar
1½ teaspoons turmeric
½ teaspoon ground cloves
1¼ cups water
2½ cups vinegar
1 tablespoon mustard seed
1 tablespoon celery seed

Combine cucumbers, onions, peppers, and salt in large bowl. Cover with 1 quart water and let stand for 3 hours. Meanwhile, in bowl, combine sugar, turmeric, and cloves, then add 1¼ cups water, vinegar, mustard seed, and celery seed. Drain salt water from vegetables and place vegetables in stockpot. Pour pickling syrup over top. Place over low heat, stirring occasionally, and bring to scalding point. Put into canning jars and seal. Yield: 10 pints.

DAVID AND MARTHA YODER, Grantsville, MD

Canning Red Beets

1½ cups brown sugar
¾ cup vinegar
2 cups red beet water

1 teaspoon salt
Beets

In saucepan, combine brown sugar, vinegar, red beet water, and salt. Heat until sugar is dissolved. Place whole or cut beets in jars. Pour sauce over them to fill jar to ½ inch from top. Put on lids and seal in hot water bath for 10 minutes.

Note: When you are cooking a large pot of red beets for canning, it doesn't need to sputter, making a big mess on your kitchen stove. Instead, cook your pot of beets in the evening on medium heat with the lid on for 10 minutes. Turn off the burner and leave the lid on until the next morning. The beets will then be soft and ready to peel and can. Remember to strain some of the red beet water and use it when you can the beets for a lovely red color.

Rebecca Huyard, Coatesville, PA

Hot Pickled Veggies

2 quarts mildly hot pepper rinds
4 quarts sweet pepper strips
2 quarts chopped cauliflower
2 quarts sliced carrots
2 quarts onion wedges
2 cups olive oil

5 cups apple cider vinegar
5 cups water
1 cup salt
2 to 3 tablespoons garlic powder
¼ cup oregano

Place hot peppers, sweet peppers, cauliflower, carrots, and onion in nonmetal container. In bowl or pitcher, mix olive oil, vinegar, water, salt, garlic powder, and oregano. Pour over vegetables. Let marinate for 24 hours. Divide into jars with tight lids. No need to seal or heat. It should keep up to a year in the refrigerator and makes a delicious addition to a meal or sandwich.

S. Beiler, Woodward, PA

Refrigerator Peppers and Onions

6 cups thinly sliced peppers
3 cups thinly sliced onion
1 quart vinegar
3 cups water

1 cup vegetable oil
¼ cup oregano
¼ cup salt

Put peppers and onion in large jar. In bowl, combine vinegar, water, oil, oregano, and salt. Pour over peppers and onion. Refrigerate. These will last a few months in the refrigerator. Excellent for sandwiches.

"A great way to use up your last garden peppers."

Emma Lynn Fisher, New Holland, PA

Coleslaw to Can

1 large head cabbage, shredded
1 cup diced celery
½ cup finely chopped onion
1 small carrot, finely chopped
2 teaspoons salt

1 teaspoon celery seed
1 teaspoon turmeric
½ teaspoon mustard powder
2 cups sugar
½ cup vinegar

In bowl, mix all ingredients together. Pack into jars. Cold pack in water bath for 10 minutes.

EDITH N. CHRISTNER, Berne, IN

Canned Pickled Eggs

Hard-boiled eggs
6 cups water
4 cups sugar

3 cups vinegar
2 tablespoons salt
1 tablespoon turmeric

Divide eggs among 7 1-quart jars, about 13 small eggs per jar. In saucepan, heat water, sugar, vinegar, salt, and turmeric. Pour over eggs. Put on lids and process in boiling water bath for 15 minutes.

"This is a good way to use up those small pullet eggs or eggs on sale. They are handy to fill out a meal or add to the table for unexpected company."

ANN SHIRK, Shiloh, OH

Barbecue Sauce

32 cups ketchup (can
   use homemade)
9 cups honey
6 cups molasses
2½ cups pineapple juice
1 cup ground mustard

½ cup garlic powder
1⅛ cup sea salt
½ cup pepper
1 cup liquid smoke
36 ounces tomato paste

Combine all in large stockpot. Simmer for 1 hour. Pour into jars with lids.
Cold pack in hot water bath for 10 minutes.

Mrs. John (Rebecca) Shetler, Lakeview, MI

Ketchup

1 gallon tomato juice
1 cup vinegar
4 cups sugar
½ teaspoon pepper

1 tablespoon salt
½ teaspoon cinnamon
¼ teaspoon cayenne pepper

In stockpot, bring tomato juice to a boil and let boil until nearly reduced to
½ gallon. Add vinegar, sugar, pepper, salt, cinnamon, and cayenne. Boil until
thickened. May take 1 hour. Put hot ketchup in jars with 2-piece lids. No
need to cold pack. Set jars upside down in storage and they will seal just fine.

Mrs. Ida Girod, Salem, IN

To Can Dry Beans

Put 1 cup dry beans in 1-quart canning jar. Add 1 teaspoon salt and fill with water. Can at 10 pounds pressure for 45 minutes. Rinse before using. Good to add to cooked soups or for baked beans.

ANNA WEAVER, Mertztown, PA

Drying Sweet Corn

Cook corn on the cob for 3 minutes. Cut off kernels and spread on flat pans to dry. Dry in oven at 250 degrees, stirring often. When completely dry, store in glass jars.

SALOMIE E. GLICK, Howard, PA

Canned Nutmeats

Put nuts in jars with 2-piece lids on. Heat jars in oven on grate at 250 degrees for 45 minutes. Turn off oven and let jars cool before removing.

MARY KAUFFMAN, Albion, PA

To Can Rice

Put 1 cup dry rice in 1-quart canning jar. Fill ¾ full with water, leaving some headspace. Add 1 teaspoon salt. Can under 10 pounds pressure for 10 minutes. Rinse and drain before using.

MRS. BETHANY MARTIN, Homer City, PA

Hearty Hamburger Soup to Can

4 pounds ground beef
2 cups chopped onion
½ cup butter
4 cups peeled and diced potatoes
4 cups shredded carrots

8 cups tomato juice
2 tablespoons salt
4 teaspoons seasoned salt
½ teaspoon pepper

In large skillet, fry beef and onion in butter until browned. In pot, cover potatoes and carrots in water and cook until almost tender. Drain. Add beef, tomato juice, salt, seasoned salt, and pepper. Pour into quart jars and secure lids. Pressure can at 11 pounds pressure for 1½ hours.

To serve: For 1 quart soup, mix together ½ cup milk and 3 tablespoons flour. Add to soup and heat thoroughly.

Mrs. Reuben N. Byler, Dayton, PA

Mom's Tomato Soup to Can

14 quarts tomatoes
14 stalks celery, chopped
14 stems parsley
14 bay leaves
2 onions, chopped
¾ cup flour

1 cup sugar or maple syrup
2 tablespoons salt
Pepper to taste
1 pound butter
1 cup heavy cream

In saucepan, cook tomatoes, celery, parsley, bay leaves, and onions until celery and onions are very tender. Run through strainer and return to saucepan. In bowl, mix flour, sugar, salt, pepper, butter, and cream into a paste. Add to tomato puree and cook for 30 minutes. Cold pack in quart canning jars for 30 minutes.

Sadie Byler, Frazeysburg, OH

CANNING RAW SAUERKRAUT

Wash and trim heads of cabbage, removing any parts that look spoiled. This is important because bad cabbage can ruin the whole batch. Shred cabbage with a Salad Master using the shoestring cone. Add 1 tablespoon sea salt per quart of cabbage. Sometimes this is guesswork as a lot of cabbage goes into a jar, but you want to be sure you have 1 tablespoon sea salt in each finished quart jar. Mix salt into cabbage and let sit in bowl for 10 minutes or until water starts to sweat from the cabbage.

Now pack cabbage into clean jars, pressing it down to bring liquid to the top of the cabbage. Leave at least 1 inch of air space in the jar. If they are too full, they will overflow during the fermenting process. Close very tightly with lids.

Lacto-fermentation is an anaerobic (without oxygen) process. The presence of oxygen once fermentation has begun will ruin the finished product. So don't remove the lids.

Keep at room temperature for 3 days, then move to your canning shelves. That's all!

It is important not to open the jars during the first 3 days. After that you can begin to eat it, but it is better as it ages. The jars may not look like they have sealed, but it still keeps. It has kept for us for more than a year. Occasionally, you will have a few spoil and it will be obvious.

Don't cook the kraut, as that kills the good bacteria that is so important in our bodies. Eating raw sauerkraut helps aid digestion and bowel health. It also builds up friendly bacteria to help fight off flu and colds easier.

Serve it out of the jar 1 to 3 times a day. Refrigerate after opening.

Rosanne Hoover, Plymouth, OH

Sauerkraut in a Jar

Pack jars tight with shredded cabbage. To quart jars, add 1 tablespoon sugar, 1½ tablespoons salt, and 1 tablespoon vinegar on top. To pint jars, add 1½ teaspoons sugar, 1 teaspoon salt, and 1½ teaspoons vinegar on top. Fill jars will boiling water and poke knife into jars so the water goes down to the bottom. Seal with tight lids (do not can). Set jars on tray and leave for 4 to 6 weeks before using.

Sadie Byler, Frazeysburg, OH

Baby Food to Can

1 part applesauce
1 part sweet potatoes, cooked and mashed
¼ part butternut squash, cooked and mashed

Mix together and pack into small jars. Cold pack for 15 minutes.

Mrs. Joseph Hochstetler, Danville, OH

Canned Bologna

50 pounds venison or beef	2 teaspoons pepper
2 pounds Tender Quick	2 pounds brown sugar
1½ ounces ground mace	½ cup liquid smoke
1½ ounces coriander powder	5 quarts warm water
1½ ounces garlic powder	1 box saltine crackers, crumbled

Mix meat and Tender Quick together. Put meat through grinder once and let stand for 24 hours. In bowl, mix mace, coriander, garlic powder, pepper, brown sugar, liquid smoke, warm water, and crackers. Mix into meat and grind again. Pack into canning jars. Seal. Cold pack for 3 hours.

David and Martha Yoder, Grantsville, MD

Liverwurst

8 to 8½ pounds hog head
    meat and scraps
2 pounds liver, cleaned
    and chunked

3 tablespoons salt
2 tablespoons pepper
¼ teaspoon cayenne
    pepper (optional)

In stockpot, cover hog heat meat and scraps with water and cook until tender. In separate pot, add liver and cover with water. Cook until tender. Drain each pot, reserving some cooking water. Grind meat together. Add salt, pepper, and cayenne. Mix well. Add cooking water just until thickness of your preference. Put into canning jars with lids. Pressure can under 10 pounds pressure for 10 minutes.

Rosina Schwartz, Salem, IN

Turkey Sausage

I like to can turkey sausage. I buy links of it in bulk when our local bulk food store has a sale. I place links into jars, put on lids with rings, and put them in a hot water bath for 3 hours. After using the sausage, there is always some broth left in the jar. I keep a container in the freezer and dump the broth in it. When I want to make soup, I just grab that broth out of the freezer and add it to my soup.

Amanda King, Honeybrook, PA

Canning Beef and Pork Chunks

Fill jars with chunks of raw meat. Add 1 teaspoon salt per quart. Fill jar with water. Can under 10 pounds pressure for 85 minutes. Makes a good broth to use with the meat.

Arlene Bontreger, Middlebury, IN

Canning Hamburger

Put raw ground beef in granite roaster. Add chopped onion and salt (1 teaspoon salt per pound of meat). Bake at 250 degrees until meat is browned. Chop it up and put in cans, packed tightly. Can under 10 pounds pressure for 30 minutes. Can be used in any recipe that calls for fried hamburger.

Arlene Bontreger, Middlebury, IN

Canning Stewing Hens

Method 1: Cut up chicken. Put whole, bone-in pieces in wide-mouth quart jars. Add 1 teaspoon salt to each jar. Seal under 10 pounds pressure for 70 minutes.

Method 2: In 16-quart canner, cover 4 whole chickens with 1½ quarts water and cook for 25 minutes. Strain. Set broth aside. Pick meat from bones. Divide meat into jars. Fill with broth. Can under 10 pounds pressure for 30 minutes. You can usually get 3 pint jars from each hen.

Arlene Bontreger, Middlebury, IN

Canned Ham in Brine

16 ounces Tender Quick
1 gallon water
16 ounces brown sugar
2 tablespoons liquid smoke
Raw sliced ham

Mix Tender Quick, water, brown sugar, and liquid smoke. Divide brine into 14 1-quart canning jars. Fill jars with ham. Cold pack for 1 hour. The brine also works for deer meat.

Rhoda Miller, Decatur, IN

Ham Cure

2 cups coarse salt
1 cup brown sugar
2 tablespoons pepper
1 tablespoon red pepper
1 tablespoon liquid smoke

In bowl, mix all ingredients. Rub well into hams and slabs of bacon. Let bacon cure for 3 to 4 days and hams for 3 to 4 weeks, then smoke to preserve.

Sadie Byler, Frazeysburg, OH

Treating Deer Meat

To remove wild flavor from venison, try this soak: Fill 5-gallon bucket ⅓ full of water. Add ½ cup vinegar, ¼ cup baking soda, and strips of deer meat. Let soak for 24 hours. Drain, rinse with clear water, drain, and grind. Preserve by freezing or canning.

Sadie Byler, Frazeysburg, OH

ALASKAN JERKY

Strips of venison, cut with the grain for chewy texture or cross grain for crisp texture
½ cup Worcestershire sauce
1 tablespoon liquid smoke
½ cup soy sauce
1 tablespoon onion powder
½ tablespoon pepper
1 tablespoon garlic powder
Red pepper flakes to taste
Tabasco sauce to taste

Put meat in glass or crockery containers. In bowl, mix Worcestershire sauce, liquid smoke, soy sauce, onion powder, pepper, garlic powder, red pepper flakes, and Tabasco sauce. Pour over meat. Marinate for 8 to 12 hours. Drain meat and put on rack in shallow baking dish. Bake at 150 degrees for 12 hours or until thoroughly dried. Store jerky in airtight container.

RUTH YODER, Berlin, PA

VENISON JERKY

3 pounds venison
1 tablespoon salt
1 teaspoon Tender Quick
1 teaspoon onion powder
1 teaspoon garlic powder
1 teaspoon pepper
¼ cup soy sauce or teriyaki sauce
⅓ cup Worcestershire sauce

Use meat that is trimmed of all fat. Cut into strips ¼ inch thick by 1 to 2 inches wide by 4 to 6 inches long. In bowl, mix salt, Tender Quick, onion powder, garlic powder, pepper, soy sauce, and Worcestershire sauce. Dip meat in sauce and layer it in glass or stainless steel pan or bowl. Pour remaining sauce over meat. Let sit for 24 to 48 hours, turning meat 1 to 2 times a day. Dry in oven at 150 to 200 degrees for about 8 hours until dried. If dried well, it will keep a long time.

MIRIAM BYLER, Spartansburg, PA

MISCELLANEOUS

"The most expensive vehicle to operate
per mile is the shopping cart."

RHODA MILLER, DECATUR, IN

Homemade Lard

Cut pork fat or beef tallow into 1-inch square cubes. Put into stainless steel canning pot. Do not fill more than ½ full so it doesn't boil over. Heat and boil until pieces stay together when pressed against side of canner. Turn off heat. Scoop pieces out with stainless steel strainer or spoon. Keep these to put in your suet feeder for the birds or give to the chickens in winter. Let the liquid fat cool awhile, then pour into glass jars with canning lids. It will keep a long time without sealing. Use for bird suet, homemade laundry soap, fried food, baking, etc.

Caution: Fat is a lot hotter than water. Keep children away. It takes a long time to cool, even when off heat. Put salt on grease fires, not water, because water will explode and spread fire. If fat starts smoking, immediately turn off heat as it can catch fire.

Miriam Byler, Spartansburg, PA

CHICKEN FAT

Place fat pieces in saucepan. Boil slowly uncovered. When reduced to liquid, you can strain. Pour into glass jars. Refrigerate. Can be used for making popcorn or frying.

ARLENE BONTREGER, Middlebury, IN

CHICKEN FEET

Make sure feet are clean. Remove skin if necessary. Simmer in water on low for a couple of hours. Strain. Use for broth.

ARLENE BONTREGER, Middlebury, IN

TURKEY BROTH

Had turkey for Thanksgiving? Be sure to save and cook the bones for broth: Put bones in stockpot; cover with water. Add celery, carrots, or bay leaf if desired. Cook on low heat for 12 hours. Strain. Can be frozen or cold packed in jars for 2½ hours. The broth makes very good gravy or soup base.

RACHEL MILLER, Millersburg, OH

Chicken Stock

1 whole free-range chicken
or 2 to 3 pounds bony
chicken parts (necks, backs,
breastbones, wings)
Gizzards (optional)
Feet (optional)
4 quarts cold water

2 tablespoons vinegar
1 large onion, coarsely chopped
2 carrots, coarsely chopped
3 celery stalks, coarsely chopped
1 bunch parsley

If using whole chicken, cut off wings and neck. Clean cavity of any fat glands. Cut chicken into several pieces. Place in stainless steel pot with water, vinegar, onion, carrots, and celery. Let stand for 30 minutes to 1 hour. Bring to a boil and remove any scum that rises to the top. Reduce heat, cover, and simmer for 6 to 12 hours. In last 10 minutes of cooking, add parsley. Remove large pieces with slotted spoon. Any pieces with meat can be cooled and the meat reserved for another recipe. Strain stock into large bowl and refrigerate until fat rises to the top. Skim off fat, and refrigerate or freeze stock until ready to use.

Benjamin Yoder Jr., Narvon, PA

Nutritious Bone Broth

Chicken bones from
2 whole birds
1 gallon water
4 large carrots, unpeeled
and with stems

4 whole stalks celery
2 large onions
1 tablespoon salt

In stockpot, place bones and water. Chop carrots, celery, and onions coarsely and add with salt. Simmer for 24 hours. Strain broth and discard bones and vegetables.

Can be taken as an immune system builder and detox aide, or added to gravies, soups, etc. Bone broth will also replace butter and oil in almost any recipe, especially when baking. It can be canned or frozen.

Lydiann Glick, Howard, PA

Chicken Batter

½ cup cornmeal
1 cup flour
1 tablespoon yeast
3 tablespoons seasoned salt

1 tablespoon pepper
2 tablespoons sugar
2 eggs
1 to 2 tablespoons lemon juice

Mix together cornmeal, flour, yeast, seasoned salt, pepper, and sugar. Set aside. In another bowl, beat eggs, then beat in lemon juice. Dip chicken pieces in egg, then roll in dry mixture. Bake or fry as desired.

MARTHA MILLER, Decatur, IN

Marinade for Steak, Chicken, or Ham

1½ cups olive oil
¾ cup coconut aminos (soy sauce replacement)
¼ cup Worcestershire sauce
¼ cup vinegar

⅓ cup lemon juice
2 cloves garlic, minced
2 teaspoons parsley
2 teaspoons dry mustard
1 teaspoon pepper

Mix all ingredients and marinate meat for at least 2 days before cooking.

BENJAMIN YODER JR., Narvon, PA

Big Mac Sauce

½ cup mayonnaise
¼ cup relish
4 tablespoons french dressing

½ tablespoon brown sugar
2 teaspoons minced onion

Mix all ingredients together and keep in refrigerator. Use on grilled burgers.

Mrs. Reuben N. Byler, Dayton, PA

Honey Mustard Sauce

1 cup mayonnaise
1½ teaspoons mustard

¼ cup brown sugar
2 tablespoons honey

Can be mixed in bowl or put in blender. Serve with chicken nuggets.

Grace Ann Miller, Big Prairie, OH

Make Your Own Vinegar

Take fresh-made cider (with tart apples is best) in amount of your choice and put it in 5-gallon bucket. Cover bucket with clean, dry cloth, and rubber band in place. Leave in warm place for a few weeks, then move to cellar for 3 to 6 months. It makes its own mother, and when it goes down to the bottom and becomes clearer, it is ready to use. You can also taste it to find out if it's ready. It can be used for baking or canning. Dilute it with water for canning as it is stronger than white vinegar.

Mrs. Lizzie N. Christner, Berne, IN

Homemade Mayonnaise

1 fresh egg
½ teaspoon salt
½ teaspoon dry mustard
¼ teaspoon paprika

1 tablespoon vinegar
1 tablespoon lemon juice
1 cup light olive oil

Blend egg, salt, dry mustard, paprika, vinegar, and lemon juice. Very slowly add oil.

RACHEL MILLER, Millersburg, OH
SARAH STUTZMAN, Homer, MI

Homemade Miracle Whip Salad Dressing

1¾ cups water
½ cup vinegar
⅔ cup flour
1 egg
¾ cup butter, softened

2 tablespoons honey
2 tablespoons maple syrup
2 teaspoons salt
1 teaspoon lemon juice
1 teaspoon mustard

In saucepan, combine water, vinegar, and flour and cook until thick. In blender, combine egg, butter, honey, maple syrup, salt, lemon juice, and mustard and blend on high until creamy. Add cooked mixture and blend on high until creamy.

Toby and Rachel Hertzler, Charlotte Court House, VA

Homemade Velveeta Cheese

1 gallon milk
2 teaspoons citric acid
¾ to 1 teaspoon baking soda
¼ cup butter

1 teaspoon salt
3 tablespoons cheddar
   cheese powder
Approximately ½ cup milk

In kettle, mix 1 gallon milk and citric acid, stirring gently until it separates. Drain off whey. Add baking soda, butter, salt, and cheese powder, mixing with curds. Add ½ cup milk. Cook while stirring briskly until lumps dissolve. Put in bowls to set. Makes a soft cheese that melts well and tastes like Velveeta.

Amanda H. Hershberger, Apple Creek, OH

Hidden Valley Ranch Mix Copycat

5 tablespoons dried
    minced onion
7 tablespoons parsley flakes

4 teaspoons dried minced garlic
1 teaspoon garlic powder

Combine ingredients and store in airtight container. For dressing: combine 2 tablespoons mix with 1 cup homemade mayonnaise and 1 cup sour cream. For dip: combine 2 tablespoons mix with 2 cups sour cream.

Sarah Stutzman, Homer, MI

Seafood Rub

3 teaspoons minced garlic
3 teaspoons onion powder
1 teaspoon dried chopped onion
2¼ teaspoons lemon pepper
2¼ teaspoons chili pepper

¾ teaspoon pepper
¾ teaspoon salt
¾ teaspoon onion salt
¾ teaspoon brown sugar
2 drops olive oil

Mix all together well and store in freezer. To use: Sprinkle on fish and bake. Or mix with breadcrumbs, dip fish in milk then in breadcrumbs to coat, and fry in butter.

LARGE BATCH MEASUREMENTS:

10 tablespoons minced garlic
10 tablespoons onion powder
3½ tablespoons dried
    chopped onion
8 tablespoons lemon pepper
8 tablespoons chili pepper

2½ scant tablespoons pepper
3 tablespoons salt
3 tablespoons onion salt
3 tablespoons brown sugar
20 drops olive oil

Miriam S. Beiler, Gap, PA

Seasoned Salt

2 cups salt
4 tablespoons pepper
½ teaspoon red pepper
1 tablespoon celery salt

1 tablespoon garlic powder
4 tablespoons onion powder
5 tablespoons paprika

Put ingredients in blender and blend until mixed together well. Use on everything you would store-bought seasoned salt like Lawry's.

Esther L. Miller, Fredericktown, OH

Taco Seasoning Mix

1 teaspoon chili powder
1 teaspoon paprika
1½ teaspoons cumin

½ teaspoon oregano
2 teaspoons parsley flakes

Mix all ingredients well. Equals the same as a store-bought package.

Mrs. Albert Summy, Meyersdale, PA

CREAM OF CHICKEN SOUP MIX

2 cups instant dry milk
1 cup cornstarch
3 tablespoons chicken soup
  base with no MSG

2 tablespoons dried
  minced onion
¼ teaspoon pepper

Mix all ingredients and store in airtight container. To equal 1 can condensed soup, mix ⅓ cup dry mix with 1¼ cups milk. Bring to a boil and stir until thickened.

Variation: Add chicken tidbits along with milk. For mushroom flavor, make mix with beef base instead of chicken and omit onion. Add diced mushrooms along with milk.

HANNAH HOCHSTETTLER, Centreville, MI

PUREED CHICKEN LIVER BABY FOOD

1 pound pastured chicken
  livers (I prefer soy free)
2 tablespoons lard
½ cup chicken stock
  or filtered water

2 tablespoons butter, softened
Approximately ½
  teaspoon sea salt

Clean membranes from livers. In skillet, sauté livers in lard until browned. Add chicken stock and boil slightly. Place in food processor and pulse until smooth. Add butter and salt. If too thick, add a bit more stock or water. The pâté should be the consistency of thick cream. Distribute among 8 small ramekins or jars. Cover with plastic wrap. Refrigerate. Use within 3 to 4 days or freeze. Before serving, heat by placing ramekin in pan of simmering water.

CHRISTINA SCHMIDT, Salem, IN

BREADCRUMBS

To make your own breadcrumbs: Use dry or stale bread, crumble onto cookie sheets, and dry on woodstove or in gas stove with pilot on. Once bread is dry, you can grind it or blend it if you have a blender. Use to coat and fry eggplant or zucchini. Season and use for chicken or whatever you wish.

DAVID AND MALINDA BEILER, Watsontown, PA

CROUTONS

Cut leftover homemade bread or stale bread with butter into cubes and spread on baking sheets. Toast in low oven, stirring every 15 minutes, or in frying pan, stirring very often. Toast until completely dried. Add seasonings while toasting if you wish, or wait until later when you decide what to use the croutons for. Good used in soups, dressing (stuffing), casseroles, or tossed salads. They keep a long time in an airtight container.

MIRIAM BYLER, Spartansburg, PA

PITA CRISPS

Split 3 pitas and cut into 8 triangles each. Place on cookie sheet and bake at 350 degrees for 10 to 12 minutes or until crisp.

TACO SHELLS

1½ cups cold water
1 cup flour
½ cup cornmeal

¼ teaspoon salt
1 egg

Mix all ingredients together until smooth. Pour ¼ scant cup batter into hot, lightly greased frying pan and rotate pan to make a nice round circle. Flip once. Serve as a wrap with meat, lettuce, cheese, onions, pickles, etc.

"These wraps are much better than the store-bought ones that are so chewy!"

RACHEL MILLER, Millersburg, OH

TORTILLA SHELLS

3 cups flour
2 teaspoons baking powder
1 teaspoon salt

4 to 6 tablespoons lard or
vegetable shortening
Approximately 1¼
cups warm water

In bowl, blend flour, baking powder, and salt. Cut in lard. You want these ingredients to cling together slightly and hold a form when squeezed. If mixture crumbles, you have too little lard. If it makes a hard clump, you have too much lard. Add water all at once and mix quickly until dough forms a mass. Work it in the bowl a bit, then knead about a dozen times to form soft dough that is no longer sticky. Let sit covered for 10 minutes for a soft tortilla. Pinch off 1-inch balls; let them sit for 10 more minutes to make them easier to handle. On floured surface, roll them to desired thickness. Cook on hot griddle or pan until puffy, flip over, and cook until done—about 30 seconds on each side. Yield: approximately 15 shells.

MRS. PERRY (REBECCA) HERSCHBERGER, Bear Lake, MI

Apple Butter

15 gallons cider
12 gallons applesauce from
  peeled and chopped
  or sliced apples

15 pounds sugar or to taste
Cinnamon to taste (optional)

In large kettle, put 9 gallons cider. Measure with yardstick or other stick where top line of cider is. Add remaining cider. Boil cider down to marked line, stirring and checking measurement occasionally. When cooked down, add applesauce and cook until thickened to your preferred consistency. Then add sugar and cinnamon. When sugar is added, it will thicken faster.

MRS. SAM B. YODER, New Wilmington, PA

Honey Butter

1 cup butter
⅓ cup honey
⅛ teaspoon cinnamon

Mix well. Spread on bread or toast.

GRACE ANN MILLER, Big Prairie, OH

Hot Butter Sauce

2 cups sugar
½ cup milk
½ cup margarine

1 egg, beaten
Vanilla to taste

In saucepan, combine sugar, milk, margarine, and egg. Bring to a boil. Add vanilla. Serve on warm cake.

S. BYLER, Reynoldsville, PA

Salted Caramel Sauce

½ cup butter
1 cup brown sugar
2 cups water

4 to 6 tablespoons Clear Jel
1 teaspoon salt
1 teaspoon vanilla

Melt butter in saucepan; add brown sugar and allow it to brown a little. Add water and bring to a boil. Mix several tablespoons Clear Jel into a little water to make a paste. Add to boiling sugar to thicken. Add salt and vanilla. Use this with date pudding. It doesn't get as soggy as traditional sauce. You can also make this recipe a little thicker and eat it with apples. It is not as sweet as most caramel sauces.

Emma Kurtz, Smicksburg, PA

Chocolate Sauce

2 squares semisweet
   chocolate, melted
½ cup butter

2 cups powdered sugar
⅔ cup evaporated milk

Combine all ingredients in saucepan and bring to a boil for 10 minutes. This sauce will harden when poured on ice cream.

Elizabeth Miller, Millersburg, OH

Peanut Butter Spread

3 pounds peanut butter
¾ pound butter

3 cups maple syrup
8 ounces cream cheese, softened

In bowl, blend peanut butter, butter, and maple syrup, mixing well. In another bowl, beat cream cheese until fluffy. Add to peanut butter mixture and mix well.

Rebecca Stoltzfus, Hagerstown, IN

Homemade Gluten-Free Baking Blend

¾ cup almond flour
½ cup flax meal
1½ cups oat fiber
1½ cups coconut flour

¾ cup whey protein isolate
2 tablespoons glucomannan or xanthan gum

If your almond flour and flax meal are coarse in texture, run them through coffee grinder to make powdery. Place all ingredients in mixing bowl and whisk together so that it is mixed well and texture is loose and fluffy. In most recipes, this blend can be substituted as 1 scant cup for each cup of all-purpose flour. It works well in cakes and muffins. Some cooks add more baking powder to help the recipe rise, but not recommended for cookies.

Mary Kauffman, Albion, PA

Gluten-Free Flour Mix

2 cups rice flour
1 cup tapioca starch
3 teaspoons xanthan gum

In mixing bowl, combine rice flour and tapioca starch. Mix in xanthan gum. Use in place of common wheat flour.

Dan and Anna Yoder, Mercer, MO

Aluminum-Free Baking Powder

½ cup cream of tartar
¼ cup cornstarch
¼ cup baking soda

Mix together and store in airtight container. Measures like store-bought.

Toby and Rachel Hertzler, Charlotte Court House, VA
Sarah Stutzman, Homer, MI

Homemade Karo Syrup

5 pounds sugar
3 cups water
½ to 1 teaspoon alum (the size of a cherry)

In stockpot, combine sugar and water and cook until clear. Add alum. Cook for 2 minutes. Remove from heat and cover. Do not remove lid until next day (about 24 hours later). Syrup will not get sugary and is nice and thick. If you want thinner syrup, add a bit more water.

Emma Kurtz, Smicksburg, PA

Sweetened Condensed Milk

1 cup evaporated cane sugar
2 cups milk
4 teaspoons cornstarch

In saucepan, combine sugar, milk, and cornstarch and bring to a boil. Boil for 5 to 7 minutes. Yield: 14 ounces.

Hannah Hochstettler, Centreville, MI

Cool Whip Substitute

2 cups heavy cream
1 tablespoon instant Clear Jel
¼ cup sugar

Whip cream until soft peaks form. Mix sugar and Clear Jel. Sprinkle over cream. Whip until desired texture.

Sarah Stutzman, Homer, MI

Raw Milk Kefir

1 tablespoon kefir grains or
1 package kefir powder
2 cups raw whole milk

½ cup good quality
cream (optional)

If using kefir grains, place them in fine strainer and rinse with filtered water. Place milk and cream in clean, wide-mouth, quart-size mason jar. If milk is cold, place in pan of simmering water until milk reaches room temperature. Add kefir grains or powder to milk, stirring well. Cover loosely with cloth and place in warm place (65 to 75 degrees) for 12 hours to 2 days.

If using powder, kefir is ready when it thickens, usually within 24 hours. If using grains, stir vigorously occasionally to distribute grains. Every time you stir, taste kefir. When it achieves tartness you like, kefir is ready. Kefir may also become thick and effervescent, depending on temperature, incubation time, and amount of grains you use. Pour kefir through strainer into another jar to remove grains. Keep grains for your next batch.

To store grains for later use, rinse well with water and place them in jar with ½ cup filtered water. They can be stored in refrigerator for several weeks or frozen for several months. If they are stored too long, though, they will lose their ability to culture milk.

Christina Schmidt, Salem, IN

COTTAGE CHEESE

Heat 1 gallon milk to exactly 190 degrees. While constantly stirring, add ½ cup apple cider vinegar. Cool to room temperature. Drain all whey out of curds. Refrigerate in tightly sealed container. To serve, add cream to amount you are going to use and it reaches desired consistency. Note: whey is excellent soil fertilizer.

SARAH STUTZMAN, Homer, MI

EASY SOUR CREAM

2 cups heavy cream
2 tablespoons plain yogurt

Stir together cream and yogurt. Set at room temperature for 12 to 15 hours or until desired thickness. Will get thicker if you put out where it is cold.

KATIE PETERSHEIM, Lakeview, MI

HOMEMADE YOGURT

2 quarts milk
1 tablespoon unflavored gelatin

2 tablespoons live, active yogurt
1 cup sugar

In saucepan, heat milk to 190 degrees. Remove from heat and let cool to 130 degrees. Meanwhile, soak gelatin in a small amount of cold water. Add yogurt and sugar to gelatin, then add to milk. Mix well with wire whisk. Place in warm area for 8 hours undisturbed. Reserve 2 tablespoons for your next batch. (To flavor, you can add some vanilla instant pudding.)

LAURA BYLER, New Castle, PA

HOUSEHOLD ADVICE
AND TIPS

God is our refuge and strength,
a very present help in trouble.

PSALM 46:1

EDITOR'S NOTES

When buying food on a limited budget, don't just go for the cheapest items available. Prioritize nutrition density and find things that will satisfy hunger for several hours. A pan full of elbow macaroni and processed cheese may look like it will feed a table full of hungry kids, but they'll likely be hungry a half hour later. Carbohydrates burn off quickly, and highly processed carbs lack the nutrition a body needs, so it sends out hunger signals again. Instead, try to put your money on proteins that will fill them up and give their bodies the nutrition they seek. For example, ground beef, canned tuna or mackerel, beans, whole fat plain yogurt or cottage cheese, unsweetened peanut butter, and so on are good proteins to build a meal on. Even better paired with a healthy fat (butter, lard, coconut oil, olive oil, etc.).

- Seek out local. Make friends with small butcher shops and farms. Often they are willing to sell meat, eggs, and produce to you cheaper than what can be found at the farmers' market and grocery stores. Particularly ask to buy their secondhand produce that isn't necessarily pretty. But if not cheaper, you can be sure of the quality you are getting when you know where it came from and decide it is worth what they are asking.

- Visit the farmers' markets and roadside stands at closing time. Often the farmer would rather sell you the produce at a deal than pack it up and take it back home.

- Find a local friend who has what you need (for example, eggs) and swap what you have (for example, homemade soap). Bartering and trading is an ancient way to do business without involving cash.

- Before shopping, check your cupboards and be sure you are not buying something you already have on hand. Also inventory what you have and be sure you are using up stored things in a timely manner. Challenge yourself to use that dusty jar of artichoke hearts before it is well past expiration date.

- Buying in bulk can save money, but only if you can use it up before it goes bad. Throwing out half a giant bag of salad greens that wilted before you could use them is often one of those hidden kitchen wastes we are ashamed to acknowledge. We all love a bargain, but it isn't saving you anything if it goes to waste.

- Shop with the seasons. Buying fruits and vegetables at the peak of their season often helps to save money. Then you can also afford to buy extra to preserve at home.

- Try growing your favorite vegetables from your own patio or backyard. A little time getting your hands dirty and patience can yield a bountiful harvest.

HARD TIMES

To survive hard times, I think the old motto holds true today: use it up, wear it out, make it do, or do without.

EMMA KURTZ, Smicksburg, PA

TRICK FOR FEEDING A CROWD

When you have several to feed and are in doubt of having enough, try using smaller than average serving spoons to make your food go farther.

RACHEL MILLER, Millersburg, OH

"This may sound wacky, but it does make a difference."

MRS. JOSEPH HOCHSTETLER, Danville, OH

Blackstrap Molasses

Blackstrap molasses is my most often used flavoring in the kitchen. Use it to add flavor and stretch coffee. Use it in place of chocolate syrup. Use it when short on cocoa for cakes and cookies. Use it instead of brown sugar in pumpkin or apple desserts by adding a little to white sugar. You can get by with half the amount of ground meat in a meatloaf if you rub blackstrap molasses into quick oats until it becomes the color of meat. You can also add seasonings like pepper, curry powder, barbecue sauce, or ketchup to the oats before combining it with the meat.

ANN SHIRK, Shiloh, OH

Deep-Fry Fat

Save your oil or fat from deep-frying for more than one use. But if the fat has a strong flavor or odor from frying strong-flavored foods, you can clarify it. Cool fat. Add a raw potato. Reheat slowly. Discard potato and strain fat. Store as usual.

MRS. ALBERT SUMMY, Meyersdale, PA

Ripe Bananas

If your bananas are getting overly ripe, peel them, put them in a freezer container, and freeze. Great for smoothies and baked goods.

BARB FISHER, Ronks, PA

Banana Peels

Rub the inside of the banana skin over mosquito and other insect bites to reduce swelling and irritation. Also works for small burns to help keep from getting infected.

MARY MILLER, Belmopan Belize, South America

Carrots

To keep carrots over winter, put a layer of garden dirt in the bottom of a 5-gallon bucket. Put a layer of unwashed carrots upright on top. Cover with a layer of garden dirt, but don't cover the tops. Store in a dark room of the basement. They should keep pretty well.

Katie Petersheim, Lakeview, MI

Celery

Regrow your celery by cutting it off a couple of inches up from the bottom of the stalk; place it in a little bowl with some water and it will grow again. Once the new roots are plentiful, plant it in the garden.

Lydia Ruth Byler, Newburg, PA

Growing Broccoli and Cabbage

Once I cut off the first head of broccoli, I leave the root part with the leaves in the ground. That will grow more broccoli throughout the summer.

After you cut a head of cabbage, leave the leaves and root. You should be able to harvest 3 to 4 small heads later.

Mrs. Joseph Miller, Navarre, OH

Parsley

Parsley can be cut again and again if you leave the roots undisturbed. But if you don't cut parsley to use, it will eventually go to seed.

Mrs. Joseph Miller, Navarre, OH

Saving Seeds

Peas – To save peas for seeds, do not pick one end of your row of peas. Once peas have dried on the plants, you can pick and shell them, having seeds for next year. You can do the same for green beans and peppers.

Tomatoes – I take a nice tomato I'm slicing to eat and remove the seeds. Place them on a paper towel and let them dry there. When ready to plant, I pick them off the towel and stick them in the dirt.

Watermelon and cantaloupe – I remove seeds from the melon we are going to eat and spread them on a paper towel to dry. When fully dried, I store them in small marked bottles. Do the same for cucumbers.

Mrs. Joseph Miller, Navarre, OH

Simple Way to Save and Start Tomatoes

Select a beautiful, large, healthy tomato. Cut a slice (or however many you want) out of the middle of the tomato. Fill a pot with garden dirt. Put the tomato slice on top. Put in storage (preferably in a cellar or cold storage area). Forget about it until spring. In February or March, bring the pot to a sunny location; add dirt on top of pot to cover seeds. Water and watch your tomatoes start to sprout. Once they are 2 inches tall, transplant to individual pots. Simple and fun!

"It is best to use heirloom tomatoes. My great-aunt, 91 years young, still does this as she has for years."

Barbie Esh, Paradise, PA

Peach Trees

Peach trees can be started from pits thrown out in the compost pile, or place pits in a pot and set them outside over winter. The pit needs to freeze before it can open up and start growing.

Mrs. Bethany Martin, Homer City, PA

SAVE EGGSHELLS

Add crushed eggshells to your row of radishes, onions, or carrots. Bugs don't like the sharp edges of the eggshells. The shells are also a good source of calcium for the garden.

LYDIA RUTH BYLER, Newburg, PA

EGGSHELL FERTILIZER

Soak eggshells 2 to 3 days in a quart jar until it develops an odor and then use the water to fertilize houseplants and other plants.

KATIE HOOVER, East Earl, PA

MRS. LEVI MILLER, Junction City, OH

BACON BREAD FOR BIRDS

Pour bacon grease over pieces of stale bread or leftover toast. Let harden. Hang from tree or bush by a string or put into a suet feeder.

MIRIAM BYLER, Spartansburg, PA

NEVER WASTE SCRAPS

Keep all your kitchen scraps for your compost pile or animals. Feed meat scraps, soft bones, and broth from meat to dogs and cats. Leftover or fresh vegetables and fruits, seeds and peelings, mashed potatoes, cooked cereal, and such can go to the chickens. Feed most anything except meat to the pigs.

MIRIAM BYLER, Spartansburg, PA

Composting

You can use cardboard boxes, newspapers, leaves, manure, bark, coffee grounds, tea bags, eggshells, fruit and vegetable trimmings, grass clippings, and vines and stalks from the garden for compost. Turn the pile every now and then to hasten decomposition. When it turns black and fluffy and smells like earth, use it in your garden and flowerbeds. Start a new pile every once in a while.

Miriam Byler, Spartansburg, PA
Mrs. Chester Miller, Centerville, PA

Mulch

Use old newspaper under mulch to keep down weeds. Mulch may be anything like grass clippings, old hay or straw, or dried leaves. I like to use aged (at least one year) horse manure mixed with sawdust bedding. Does a great job in flowerbeds.

Mrs. Bethany Martin, Homer City, PA

Orange Peels

Dry your orange peels and use in air freshener sachets. Or simmer on stove with cinnamon sticks, whole cloves, lemons, etc. for a delicious smell during winter months. You can also grind dried orange peels and mix with your cow's feed.

Mrs. Levi Miller, Junction City, OH

Citrus Cleaner

Save lemon, orange, or grapefruit peels. Fill a jar ⅔ full of citrus peels, fill with vinegar, and let sit for 2 to 4 weeks. Strain out the peels and put liquid in a spray bottle. You can add lemon or tea tree oil for added strength. Makes a good cleaner.

Lydia Ruth Byler, Newburg, PA

Butter Wrappers

Keep wrappers from butter sticks. Fold in half and store in the refrigerator. Use them to grease baking pans.

Miriam Byler, Spartansburg, PA

Cheap Waxed Paper

If you buy cereal in boxes, save the bags and use in place of waxed paper. If you layer freshly baked cookies in a plastic storage container, it works well instead of using waxed paper. It is much stronger, but it cannot be used for baking like regular waxed paper.

Mrs. Levi Miller, Junction City, OH

FIRE STARTERS

Fill an egg carton loosely with wood shavings. Pour melted candle wax or paraffin over the shavings. Let harden and break into pieces and use to start a fire.

Mrs. Levi Miller, Junction City, OH

SALT WATER

After you are finished freezing ice cream, pour the salt water on your asparagus and rhubarb patch. It will help kill weeds and your plants will love it.

Mrs. Levi Miller, Junction City, OH

RAGS

Cut up old T-shirts, long johns, socks, and the like to use as rags. When cleaning yucky messes, just dispose of the rag with the mess. For regular cleaning or water messes, you can throw the rags in with the laundry. This greatly saved on using paper towels.

Miriam Byler, Spartansburg, PA

SALVAGING OLD SHEETS

If the middle of a sheet is worn out, use the sides to make pillowcases, hankies, and more.

Rosie Schwartz, Salem, IN

Soap Markers

Dry small slivers of bar hand soap once they are too small to use. Use them to mark off patterns for clothes or to put a pattern on a quilt with a stencil. Works best on dark or bright-colored fabric.

Mrs. Levi Miller, Junction City, OH

Sorghum Molasses

When sorghum molasses is too old for use in cooking and baking, drizzle it over the cows' and horses' feed. It's a good source of iron and minerals for them.

Mrs. Levi Miller, Junction City, OH

Homemade Vitamins

Carrots

Peppers

Broccoli

Green beans

Whole red beet plants

100% vodka Glycerin

Very finely chop up equal parts of each vegetable. Put in glass jar. Cover vegetables with half and half mixture of 100% vodka and glycerin. Shake every day for 4 weeks. Strain and bottle. Take by spoonful. Very good to prevent colds, flu, etc.

Lovina Gingerich, Dalton, OH

Deodorant

¼ cup organic coconut oil
1 tablespoon beeswax
¼ cup baking soda
¼ cup cornstarch

1 tablespoon arrowroot powder
6 drops essential oil of choice
8 drops tea tree oil

Put some water in saucepan. Put coconut oil and beeswax in canning jar and place in saucepan of water. Heat water to melt oil over low heat. Add baking soda, cornstarch, arrowroot powder, essential oil, and tea tree oil to jar and mix well. Pour mixture into little jars and let sit for several hours to solidify. Apply with fingertips.

SADIE BYLER, Frazeysburg, OH

Baby Wipes

1 roll paper towels
2 cups boiling water

3 tablespoons baby bath wash
2 tablespoons baby oil

Cut paper towel roll in half. Remove center cardboard. Place half roll upright in airtight container. Mix boiling water, bath wash, and baby oil. Pour over roll. Cover tightly. Ready to use in 1 hour. Wipes can be pulled up from the center. Just tear off what you need. Works as well as store-bought ones.

ISAAC SCHWARTZ, Stanwood, MI

Shampoo

Flake 1 bar castile soap. In saucepan, melt soap in 1 pint boiling water, then cool. Put soap mixture in bowl and add 1 egg. Beat with beater. Pour in jar. After it has settled, it is ready to use. This shampoo will keep fine on the bathroom shelf.

TOBY AND RACHEL HERTZLER, Charlotte Court House, VA

Bleach Alternative

1½ cups 3% hydrogen peroxide
½ cup lemon juice
Water to fill 1-gallon jar

Mix ingredients and store in glass jar. Use 1 cup solution per load of laundry.

Mary Ellen Stoltzfus, Gap, PA

Homemade Laundry Soap

4 pounds clean lard
1½ cups lye
2 quarts cold water

½ cup Borax
1 cup powdered laundry detergent

In stainless steel bowl, mix lard and lye. No need to melt the lard or dissolve the lye. Stir well. Add water and stir. It will become hot from the chemical reaction. Add Borax and detergent. Keep stirring until thick. Pour into glass or stainless steel pans. Let sit awhile, then cut into bars. You can grate it if you want to or just use a bar. Dissolve soap in hot water to do your laundry.

Caution: Lye will cause severe burns if eaten or gotten on skin, until it is dried and cured. I like to let it sit quite awhile to dry out so that it won't burn the hands.

Miriam Byler, Spartansburg, PA

Fabric Softener

To save money, you can dilute fabric softener by half with white vinegar. By the time your clothes are dry, they will smell fresh and clean with no scent of vinegar.

Add 1 ounce lavender oil to 1 gallon white vinegar. You can put it right into the gallon of vinegar. You have an instant fabric softener. Shake well before each use. Add ½ to 1 cup to your rinse water.

Mrs. Dan L. E. Miller, Dayton, PA

PLAY DOUGH

2 cups flour
4 teaspoons cream of tartar
1 cup salt

2 cups water
3 tablespoons vegetable oil
Food coloring

In saucepan, mix flour, cream of tartar, and salt. Add water, oil, and a few drops food coloring. Cook over medium heat, stirring constantly until very stiff, about 2 to 3 minutes. Cool slightly, then knead for a few minutes.

"Hours of fun for preschoolers!"

ALLEN AND SUSAN RABER, Sugarcreek, OH

Tin Cans

Recycle your tin cans to make cute buckets. Gallon, half-gallon and quart cans make great buckets for children to carry water. Punch 2 holes in the top and fasten a strong wire to make a handle.

Use a tin can with a sharp edge as a Quick Chop. Or use them to collect bugs off plants.

Short cans can be used to make pin cushions. Crochet a bowl the same size as your tin. Slip it over the tin, leaving the top open. Fill the bowl with a good amount of hair that you combed out. Cut a cloth the right size for the top and tightly stitch it onto the yarn. The tin is covered, and you have a place for your pins. The hair keeps the pins rust-free.

Mrs. Levi Miller, Junction City, OH

Index of Contributors

INDEX OF RECIPES BY SECTION

Main Dishes

Desserts

HOUSEHOLD ADVICE AND TIPS

Index of Recipes by Key Ingredients

OTHER COOKBOOKS BY
WANDA AND HER FRIENDS

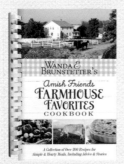

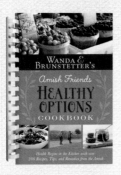

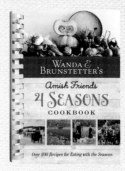

Wanda E. Brunstetter's Amish Friends **Farmhouse Favorites** *Cookbook*

Wanda E. Brunstetter's Amish Friends **From Scratch** *Cookbook*

Wanda E. Brunstetter's Amish Friends **Healthy Options** *Cookbook*

Wanda E. Brunstetter's Amish Friends **Baking** *Cookbook*

Wanda E. Brunstetter's Amish Friends **4 Seasons** *Cookbook*